"Some books simply stand out from the rest because they grab your attention the moment you see the title. And then there are the very, very few that also keep you riveted page after page. *50 Ideas that Changed the World of Work* is a fitting testimony to the shoulders on whom we can stand to see better. A book whose time has come."
—Sudhanshu Palsule, leadership philosopher, educator, coach, and speaker

"An insightful and practical compendium of the key ideas shaping workplace practices over the past half-century or so. It is essential reading for anyone wishing to bring best practice to their organisation."
—Andy Haldane, chief executive, Royal Society of Arts (RSA)

"In turbulence, you want a solid guide. This collection of 50 key concepts supports clear thinking with simplicity and direction."
—Professor Nandani Lynton, global head of change and culture, SAP

"A wonderful toolkit that will save you years of reading and workshops. It not only summarises each idea in a very easy read, but specifies how to put the idea into practice and poses questions you will need to ask yourself to place the idea into your own context. I'm keeping this one in my rucksack wherever I go!"
—Adam Kingl, author, keynote speaker, educator

"A terrific book; a fantastic collection of essential models and theories from great thinkers, presented in an accessible and bite-sized way that says, 'read me.'"
—Jerome Goodluck, senior business manager, The Institute of Leadership

"A cornucopia of inspirational resources for leaders of all levels."
—Russell Beck, managing director, ImagineThinkDo Ltd and author of *The World of Work to 2030*

"In a world where leaders are looking for a silver bullet, it is refreshing to find a book bold enough to look back at the tremendous research and work done over many years. I applaud the authors for their willingness to admit that much great work has already been created—and we run the risk of ignoring it if we only look at the shiny new books on the shelf. I encourage any leader or aspiring leader to dive into this book to identify many golden nuggets to support your growth."

—Roger Minton, former head of leadership
development, Anglo American

"An incredible compendium of ideas, presented in an engaging way so you can immediately put them into practice. From timeless classics to recent breakthroughs, the ideas in this book will help you to think more strategically, transform your culture, reset priorities, boost relationships and understand yourself better. All the most important insights together in one easy-to-read book. Highly recommended."

—Mark Williamson, director and co-founder of Action for
Happiness

"I wish I'd had this book through my entire professional career. How much time and stress I would have saved. It should be recommended reading for every business professional, no matter their function or level."

—Pepe González Tejera, executive education expert and former
VP global marketing and business development, Tetra Pak

"As a transformational expert, I understand the challenges of navigating a fast-changing world—from technological disruption and geopolitical instability to climate action and hybrid working. This book provides invaluable insights into the ideas that have shaped the modern workplace and offers practical inspiration for leading transformation."

—Araceli Canedo Bebbington, executive coach and board
member, The European Mentoring and Coaching Council

50 IDEAS
THAT CHANGED THE WORLD OF WORK

The Essential Guide to the
Best Business Thinking

Jeremy Kourdi & Jonathan Besser

50 IDEAS THAT CHANGED THE WORLD OF WORK

Published with permission from *The Economist* by Pegasus Books.

The Economist is an imprint of
Pegasus Books, Ltd.
148 West 37th Street, 13th Floor
New York, NY 10018

Copyright © 2025 by Jeremy Kourdi and Jonathan Besser

First Pegasus Books cloth edition June 2025

All rights reserved. No part of this book may be reproduced in whole or in part without written permission from the publisher, except by reviewers who may quote brief excerpts in connection with a review in a newspaper, magazine, or electronic publication; nor may any part of this book be reproduced, stored in a retrieval system, or transmitted in any form or by any means electronic, mechanical, photocopying, recording, or other, or used to train generative artificial intelligence (AI) technologies, without written permission from the publisher.

ISBN: 978-1-63936-849-5

10 9 8 7 6 5 4 3 2 1

Printed in the United States of America
Distributed by Simon & Schuster
www.pegasusbooks.com

PEGASUS BOOKS
NEW YORK LONDON

With thanks to the brilliant thinkers, past
and present, whose bold and insightful work
continues to support and inspire us all.

Thanks as well to the readers who apply these ideas –
shaping and improving what we do and how we do it.

About the authors

Jeremy Kourdi is a business writer, executive coach, educator and founder of Expert Leader. He was formerly Senior Vice President of *The Economist*, Managing Director of Duke Corporate Education, and Head of Publishing and Research at the UK's Chartered Management Institute. Jeremy's experience includes coaching, leadership development and thought leadership with a wide range of market-leading organisations and business schools. He is the author of 30 books, translated into 17 languages, and has in-depth expertise in the fields of leadership, coaching, innovation and the forces shaping the future for business and society.

Jonathan Besser is an internationally experienced learning and development expert, as well as a coach, mentor and facilitator. He is the founder of Intrepid Leadership Consulting and works with clients across a wide range of industries – from engineering, finance and fast-moving consumer goods to professional services, media, advertising and manufacturing. Jonathan believes in collaborative partnership and puts it at the heart of everything he does. His work embraces the evolving nature of learning and technology, and he is experienced in a wide range of learning interventions and tools. He has worked with market-leading business schools and consultancies around the world, providing leadership development and getting involved in all aspects of client work, including programme design, diagnostics, development and delivery.

Contents

Introduction	1
1. Thinking, fast and slow	3
2. Emotional intelligence	7
3. Neuro-linguistic programming	13
4. Growth mindset	17
5. Psychological safety	22
6. The GROW model of coaching	27
7. The Myers-Briggs Type Indicator	33
8. Luft and Ingham's Johari window	40
9. Csikszentmihalyi's *Flow*	46
10. VUCA: volatility, uncertainty, complexity and ambiguity	51
11. Black swans	55
12. Scenario planning	59
13. Ambidexterity	63
14. Kotter's eight steps for leading change	69
15. The Eisenhower matrix	75
16. Covey's seven habits of highly effective people	81
17. Sun Tzu's *The Art of War*	85
18. Blue ocean strategy	90
19. Porter's five forces: competitive strategy	95
20. The business model canvas	101
21. SWOT and PEST analysis	107
22. The shamrock organisation	113
23. Kaizen and business process re-engineering	118
24. Systems thinking and the critical path	123
25. The balanced scorecard	128

26. Doblin's *Ten Types of Innovation* — 135
27. Disruptive innovation — 141
28. The growth share matrix — 147
29. Product life cycle model — 152
30. Net Promoter Score — 158
31. Kotler's four Ps of marketing — 163
32. Gladwell's tipping point — 169
33. Lewin's leadership styles — 173
34. Situational leadership — 178
35. Charan's leadership pipeline — 183
36. Belbin team roles — 189
37. Tuckman's stages of team development — 194
38. Hackman's enabling conditions for teams — 199
39. SMART goal setting — 204
40. Maslow's hierarchy of needs — 209
41. Schein's three levels of organisational culture — 215
42. Sandberg's *Lean In* — 221
43. The Thomas–Kilmann conflict model — 225
44. Scott's *Radical Candor* — 231
45. Giving great feedback — 238
46. Cialdini's principles of ethical influence and persuasion — 242
47. Appreciative inquiry — 248
48. Carnegie's *How to Win Friends and Influence People* — 253
49. Maister's trust equation — 258
50. Win–win negotiation — 263

Acknowledgements — 269
Bibliography, further reading and resources — 271
Index — 281

Introduction

As we hurtle through the third decade of the 21st century it would be fair to say that the challenges facing organisations appear to be relentless and unprecedented: pandemics, conflict, technological change, political and economic upheaval, and more. But spare a thought for Kongō Gumi, a Japanese construction company that can trace its origins back to 578 AD. That's over 1,400 years of change and turmoil. In the Western world we have many global businesses that have been trading for well over 100 years including IBM, Merck, Coca-Cola, Kellogg's, Kraft, Harley-Davidson and Rolls-Royce. These are businesses that have succeeded and survived with experience and resilience, often influencing (and being influenced by) the thinking, models and techniques that have informed what, how and why we do what we do at work today.

Although the challenges we face today might feel new to us, they might not be new to the world of business. That's why, for this book, we've chosen to look back, researching and studying 50 ideas that have changed the world of work for the better. These are ideas and initiatives that have been created to address problems at a moment in time and have proved so useful that we still use them today in their original or adapted form.

This thinking has a long history. Frederick Winslow Taylor wrote his ground-breaking book *The Principles of Scientific Management* in 1911, producing a work that was hugely influential for everyone from Henry Ford to Peter Drucker – people who were themselves great influencers.

As a starting point, it's interesting to consider Taylor's original four principles.

1. Replace approximation, guesswork and intuition with a fact-based approach based on a scientific study of the work to be completed.
2. Carefully invest in selecting, training, developing and promoting employees, rather than allowing them to learn, train and improve themselves passively.
3. Ensure that each individual employee receives detailed, coordinated instruction and supervision of their work.
4. Plan and divide work fairly and in the most operationally effective way, particularly between managers and workers, and work together to complete the necessary tasks.

More than 110 years later, few would disagree with Taylor's observations and recommendations.

In a world where thousands of new business books are published every year, it may seem counterintuitive to look back. But, as we have discovered, much of what we do in our organisations today can be directly linked to models that were created decades ago.

There are, of course, many more than 50 ideas that have changed the world of work. We have chosen 50 of the most interesting, potent, popular or practical. Some are newer ideas; some are older foundational ideas; all are relevant today and will remain relevant into the future. You might think of the book as a business thinking equivalent of an anthology of poetry, a companion and guide designed to whet your appetite for delving deeper.

We have designed each entry to be clear and succinct, distilling the essence of each idea: what it means and why it matters. Crucially, we have taken a practical approach so that these ideas can be applied as quickly and easily as possible. That is what lies behind the "In practice" section and the questions posed in each chapter's "Thought starters".

We encourage you to use these insights to strengthen your capabilities and develop your thinking about the world of work and to create the sustained, positive change that makes for better organisations.

Jeremy Kourdi and Jonathan Besser

1

Thinking, fast and slow

Understanding the science of decision making

The big picture

In his 2011 book *Thinking, Fast and Slow*, Israeli-American Nobel laureate and psychologist Daniel Kahneman explored how we make decisions. In doing so he provided practical insights into neuroscience and how our brains work, bringing to life the concept of fast and slow thinking as two parallel systems of thought that operate in the human mind. Kahneman defined System 1 thinking as automatic, intuitive and emotional; System 2 thinking as slower, more deliberate and logical. By understanding these two systems you can become more aware of how you make decisions and how you can improve your decision-making processes.

Kahneman's work has affected many people's understanding of decision-making, neuroscience and behavioural psychology. This includes greater awareness of the role of intuition, the limitations of judgements based on hindsight, and the impact of money and other subtle influences and biases on decision-making.

About the idea

Fast and slow thinking refers to the idea that there are two parallel systems of thought that operate in the human mind.

Fast thinking

Fast thinking, or System 1, involves automatic and intuitive thinking that occurs without much effort. It is responsible for things like perception, attention, and basic cognitive tasks such as knowing how to tie our shoelaces or being able to do simple arithmetic, like 2+2. System 1 thinking is often automatic and is the source of our gut reactions and snap judgements. It works very well for many of the decisions that need to be made "in the moment" and every moment of every day. If people were to engage System 2, or slow thinking, for every decision made, it would be cognitively overwhelming and time consuming.

The key is to know when to slow down, to take a breath, and engage System 2 in your processing.

Slow thinking

Slow thinking, or System 2, involves more deliberate, reflective and logical thinking requiring effort and concentration. It is responsible for things like problem-solving, decision-making and higher-order thinking. System 2 thinking is more considered and is used when there is a need to override the intuitive System 1 responses or when faced with complex problems. If you were asked, for example, to multiply 17 by 24, you would struggle to come up with an answer using only System 1 thinking.

People can learn to recognise when they are relying too much on fast, intuitive System 1 thinking and not using slower, more deliberate System 2 thinking enough. You can also learn to identify situations where you need to override System 1 responses and engage System 2 thinking to make more thoughtful and reasoned decisions.

Understanding fast and slow thinking can help you to become a more intentional and effective decision-maker, helping you to acknowledge and understand when going with your instinct might not lead to the best outcomes or how bias might affect the decisions you make. Kahneman's work provides a valuable focus for enhanced self-awareness and his concepts are often reflected in training programmes, coaching discussions, and simply in the way that people work.

In practice

There are several ways to apply Kahneman's concept of fast and slow thinking.

Take time to reflect on how you make key decisions

When faced with a tricky or complex decision, try to slow down and take time to engage your slower, more deliberate System 2 thinking. Ask yourself questions like: what are the options and their pros and cons? What is the goal or priority? What are the potential long-term consequences of this decision (or of not making a decision)?

Be careful, however, not to overthink decisions, perhaps because of an excess of caution or "paralysis by analysis". If you're facing a System 1 decision, the best approach is to get on with making it happen.

Be aware of your biases and mental shortcuts

Everyone has biases and shortcuts that influence their thinking and decisions. These might be a tendency towards stereotyping or being overly influenced by recent events (recency bias). By being aware of these you can make decisions that are more objective, balanced and informed.

Practise mindfulness

One way to engage your slower, more reflective System 2 thinking is through mindfulness practices such as meditation or writing down your feelings. These practices can help you become more aware of your thoughts and emotions and develop a more balanced and rational perspective.

Seek out diverse perspectives

When faced with a complex problem, try to gather input from people with different backgrounds, experiences, expertise and viewpoints. This can help you to see the problem from different angles and produce more creative solutions.

Take breaks and rest

When feeling overwhelmed or tired it can be difficult to engage your slower, more reflective System 2 thinking. Taking breaks and getting enough rest can help you to recharge and be more effective in your problem-solving and decision-making.

Thought starters

- When and how often does your automatic System 1 thinking influence your decisions and actions? Can you remember occasions when your gut reactions led you astray?
- In what situations do you tend to rely more on your slower, more deliberate System 2 thinking?
- Consider how you can make the time and space to engage more thoughtful System 2 thinking.
- How aware are you of your cognitive biases?
- How can you apply the concept of fast and slow thinking to problem-solving? What more can you do to engage your slower, more reflective System 2 thinking when faced with complex problems?

What next?

Read *Thinking, Fast and Slow* by Daniel Kahneman.

2

Emotional intelligence

How to manage and deploy emotions effectively

The big picture

Psychologist Daniel Goleman popularised the concept of emotional intelligence in his 1995 bestselling book *Emotional Intelligence: Why It Can Matter More Than IQ*. Building on the work of Howard Gardner, Peter Salovey and John Mayer, Goleman highlighted the fact that recognising, understanding and deploying emotions effectively is a precursor to personal and organisational success, and can be especially important in times of change, pressure or crisis. For example, we may all feel anger, but emotional intelligence helps us deploy that anger (or not) to achieve the best outcome.

The rise in popularity and impact of emotional intelligence reflects the embrace of psychology in the world of work as well as another, closely related phenomenon: the recognition that understanding and getting the best from people holds the key to many of the most challenging tasks confronting people at work.

For example, if you want to appeal to new and existing customers and employees, learn and adapt to changing circumstances, thrive in times of crisis, innovate, work effectively in teams, make the most effective decisions, then a positive environment with people working effectively together is indispensable. People are essentially social animals; harnessing this socialisation is the real benefit of emotional intelligence.

About the idea

In his book, Daniel Goleman developed a framework of five elements that define emotional intelligence.

Understanding one's emotions and being self-aware

Although people's moods often influence their thoughts, people only occasionally pay attention to the way they feel. This is significant because previous emotional experiences provide a context for decisions and actions. Being aware of your feelings and being able to manage them affects impulse control, personal development, confidence and self-belief. People with high emotional intelligence are typically self-aware: they are better able to avoid blind spots and can understand (and mitigate) their biases. (See Chapter 8.)

Managing emotions: self-regulation and control

Emotionally intelligent people know or learn how to control their impulses and emotions, especially the big three: anger, anxiety and sadness. This emotional resilience enables people to perform consistently in a range of situations, even when under pressure, and to adapt their behaviour as needed. Self-control means they are able to avoid impulsive, careless decisions. Characteristics of self-regulation include thoughtfulness, being comfortable with ambiguity and change, displaying integrity and being able to say no.

Motivating yourself

Emotionally intelligent people are usually motivated and understand what gives them focus, energy and enjoyment. Motivated people typically defer immediate results for longer-term success and are productive, resilient and effective at overcoming challenges. This in turn puts them in a better position to motivate others – for example, by sharing their own motivations and by providing examples of the benefits of motivation.

Displaying empathy and recognising emotions

Self-awareness is sometimes seen as the most important component of emotional intelligence, but empathy is a close second. People with empathy can sense and recognise the feelings of others, even when those feelings may not be obvious. As a result, they are successful at building relationships by actively listening and finding sincere ways to relate to others. This then provides a strong foundation for a range of other work activities, from teamworking to selling. Crucially people with a high degree of empathy avoid stereotyping and judging others too quickly, and are open, honest and effective relationship-builders.

Developing social skills and building relationships

Goleman makes the point that personal emotions are contagious and that there is an invisible transaction between individuals in every interaction, making them feel either better or worse. Goleman refers to this as a "secret economy" and believes it holds the key to building better relationships at work. Individuals who excel in this area typically focus on the success of others before themselves, making them great team players, coaches and managers. They are adept at resolving disputes, communicating, influencing and engaging people, and the relationships they build tend to endure.

In practice

Emotional intelligence can be learned and strengthened by focusing on Goleman's five domains.

Develop self-awareness

To increase self-awareness, spend time understanding and decoding your emotions and how you typically feel and behave. For example, when do you get upset? What triggers you? How do you typically react?

It also helps to observe how you react to other people, and how well you understand their emotional states. Consider your work environment and what would be helpful in that context. For example, would you benefit from more or less humility; greater confidence or more controlled confidence; or an enhanced ability to work with others?

Manage emotions

Emotional resilience can be achieved in several ways. First, name the emotions that are dominant for you, and note when you use them. Next, consider and, if possible, discuss the emotional qualities you would like to develop. Naming emotions – being clear and explicit about what they are as well as how and when they manifest for you – is vital for understanding and deploying them effectively.

Other actions that can help build emotional resilience include evaluating your strengths and areas for development; assessing how you react to stressful situations and how this could improve; understanding how effectively you take responsibility for your actions, especially when you make mistakes; and being honest about how your behaviour affects others.

Motivate yourself and others

Significantly, the ability to motivate and engage others starts with self-motivation. To enhance personal motivation, therefore, consider what gives you energy and enjoyment, and what causes you despondency, frustration or anger. What situations and people bring out the best in you, and when are you at your most vulnerable or ineffective?

It also helps to understand what would improve your ability to balance short- and long-term goals, and to stay the course in the face of challenges or setbacks. How can you increase your confidence, resilience and likelihood of success?

Levels of motivation are typically enhanced with action in several areas – for example, by working with people who are highly motivated, setting realistic but challenging targets, and taking time to acknowledge progress and success. Progress is a great motivator, along with recognition and reward.

Develop greater empathy

Empathy is the ability to identify with and understand the wants, needs and viewpoints of those around you. It can be enhanced simply by getting into the habit of asking yourself how you would feel in the same situation. You can also build empathy by developing the habit of asking people for their views and actively listening by giving them your full attention and exploring with them what they say and why. Another valuable habit is taking time to reflect on how someone is saying something, why they are saying it that way, and what they are not saying.

Build relationships

Goleman emphasises the value of developing strong, warm relationships at work and elsewhere. Without the connection, openness and understanding that comes from emotional intelligence you are more likely to encounter misunderstanding, fear, blame or isolation. Several actions and habits can help. These include being open and sharing a little of yourself – for example, how you feel, what you intend, how you can help.

Take the time to build rapport. Genuinely enquiring how someone feels or what is going on in their life can go a long way to building a connection and showing your positive intent. Rapport matters, because the connection that it provides gives you the foundation on which to build a relationship, to challenge, for example, or to influence. Open, constructive questioning will generate understanding and lead to relationships that are deeper and more robust.

Thought starters

- What are your dominant emotions, and what impact might they have on your decisions and actions?
- Think about who in your organisation is good at demonstrating empathy. How do they show it?

- What motivates you? What can you do to build your levels of energy and motivation?
- Are you always sufficiently sensitive to others? How could you improve your understanding of other people?
- Do you take time to build rapport and relationships? Are you sufficiently open and ready to engage with others? What more could you do to build relationships?

What next?

Read *Emotional Intelligence: Why It Can Matter More Than IQ* by Daniel Goleman.

3
Neuro-linguistic programming

The connections between language, thought and behaviour

The big picture

Developed in the 1970s from extensive studies by Richard Bandler and John Grinder, neuro-linguistic programming (NLP) is a psychological approach that helps people understand the relationship between language, behaviour and thought; how they can be used to support effective communication and personal change, and to achieve specific goals.

One of the key principles of NLP is the idea that individuals have the power to change their own thoughts and behaviours. By understanding and consciously modifying these patterns they can improve their communication and influence, achieve personal and professional goals, and create the life they want.

As a result, NLP techniques are often used in coaching, training and development as well as therapy, and are designed to help individuals identify and change negative thoughts and behaviours that may be holding them back.

About the idea

NLP uses a variety of techniques.

- *Language patterns* to influence how others perceive and respond to a message.
- *Reframing* – changing the way people think about or interpret a situation to see it in a more positive and productive light.

- *Anchoring* or creating a physical or emotional trigger that can be used to access a desired state or behaviour.
- *Modelling* – by analysing and replicating the behaviour and language patterns of successful individuals to achieve similar results.
- *Visualisation* – using mental imagery to help people see themselves achieving their goals and stay motivated.
- *Goal setting* – identifying and setting clear, achievable goals using techniques such as visualisation and anchoring to help stay focused and motivated.
- *Time management* strategies and ways of setting priorities.

At work, NLP techniques are used to improve communication skills, overcome problems and barriers, achieve goals and improve relationships with colleagues and clients.

There are concerns that NLP lacks a robust scientific underpinning or could be used to manipulate people. Despite this, it has endured and succeeded in a wide range of settings since the 1970s, such as reframing situations to help individuals see them in a more positive and productive light, and building trust and rapport through effective communication.

In practice

NLP helps people change the way they think and act in several ways: focusing on the words and phrases being used (for example, avoiding jargon), changing the way people respond to events, and helping them learn new habits.

It typically starts with identifying the specific goal you would like to achieve. This may be an end goal such as attaining a promotion, or a performance goal – for example, improving communication skills.

Depending on your goal, choose and apply the most appropriate NLP technique.

For example, you may want to work in another department or function but lack the confidence to apply for a role. Using visualisation techniques to imagine what the role would be like and how you would fulfil your new responsibilities might help to demystify it. You might also use anchoring techniques to overcome any anxiety related to lack of confidence. Together, these NLP techniques can help you to reframe the situation as an achievable goal, rather than seeing it as being beyond your reach.

NLP at work can also help you in other practical ways.

Improve communication skills

NLP techniques such as being more aware of language patterns and framing can help people communicate more effectively. This might involve improving active listening, using appropriate body language (and possibly mirroring the other person's body language), and using language that is clear, concise and easy to engage with.

Overcome challenges

People can identify and overcome challenges or obstacles that are holding them back by using NLP techniques like identifying negative thoughts and the triggers or situations that prompt them, as well as the behaviours that are contributing to the challenge, and then developing new strategies for dealing with them. This requires good self-awareness (see Chapter 2) to understand your emotions and behaviour in particular circumstances, and how they affect your self confidence and behaviours.

Achieve goals

NLP can help people set and achieve goals. This is achieved by encouraging visualisation: developing a clear vision of what needs to be accomplished, what it would mean, why it matters, how it would feel to achieve the goal, and the actions needed to ensure success. Techniques such as anchoring and reframing can help maintain focus and motivation.

Improve relationships

Learning how to communicate more effectively, developing empathy and connection, and building trust and rapport can help you to improve relationships with colleagues, clients and other stakeholders.

For example, you might consider using storytelling techniques in presentations. Instead of delivering dry, factual information – essentially talking "at" people – it is much better to share a story that will both deliver the key message and be engaging for the audience.

Thought starters

- Consider whether your language, behaviour or thoughts sometimes hold you back from achieving a goal. What could you change?
- What elements of NLP could you use to overcome perceived obstacles?
- What new habits could you adopt? How could you improve your influence within your organisation?
- How could visualisation and reframing help to improve the performance of your team?

What next?

Read *Reframing: Neuro-Linguistic Programming and the Transformation of Meaning* by Richard Bandler and John Grinder.

4

Growth mindset

Finding the upside of challenge and change

The big picture

Carol Dweck, a professor of psychology at Stanford University, is known for her thinking about the importance of what she calls *growth mindset* – the belief that talent and capability can be developed through curiosity, learning and input from others. Dweck distinguishes this approach from a *fixed mindset* held by people who believe that people are innately gifted and talented (or not) and are therefore less open to opportunities to develop themselves.

Dweck's ideas gained significance and popularity with the publication in 2006 of her book *Mindset: The New Psychology of Success*. Driving this has been a widespread need for new ways to think about uncertainty, unfamiliar challenges and constant change manifested since then by examples as wide ranging as the covid-19 pandemic, economic volatility and the impact of climate change.

The 21st century has delivered volatile, unfamiliar and shocking black swan events (see Chapter 11), often with challenging and largely unknowable consequences. It is against this backdrop of volatility that individuals and organisations have increasingly come to view a *growth mindset* as a route to progress or, at least, as an indispensable tool for survival.

About the idea

Central to the concept of a growth mindset is the idea that people's approach to life and work – their mindset – is either fixed, with intelligence remaining static (at best); or is dynamic and growth-oriented, rooted in the belief that intelligence can be developed.

The difference between the two mindsets can be seen most clearly in five key areas:

- when facing challenges
- encountering obstacles
- deciding how much effort to apply
- handling criticism
- responding to the success of others.

Fixed mindset

People with a fixed mindset typically view the current version of themselves as being the best, the finished article. This static approach leads to a desire or need to be regarded as intelligent. As a result, people with a fixed mindset are more likely to avoid challenges, give up in the face of obstacles, see effort as pointless, reject criticism, and feel threatened by the success of others. The inevitable outcome is that they plateau, fail to progress and achieve less than their potential.

Growth mindset

People with a growth mindset believe that intelligence and skills can and should be developed. This leads to a fundamental desire to learn and improve, which results in a desire to embrace challenges, persist in the face of setbacks, see effort as necessary to progress and improvement, learn from criticism, and find lessons and inspiration from the success of others. As a direct consequence of a growth mindset, they are better placed to make progress and achieve success in a fast-changing world.

The growth mindset resonates with people in a wide range of situations. Examples include the businesses who used the covid-19 pandemic as a way to increase innovation and flexibility, and individuals unsuccessful in job applications who react positively by reframing the setback as an opportunity to do something else. In sport, players can adapt their style to suit new opponents and tactics. Architects learn from nature and science to overcome engineering challenges. In politics, when Winston Churchill was working to form the United Nations after the Second World War, he famously said: "Never let a good crisis go to waste." All are examples of a growth mindset.

In practice

Carol Dweck emphasises two significant points for anyone looking to develop a growth mindset. First, nobody has a 100% fixed or a 100% growth mindset at any point. People are somewhere along this continuum and your approach might change depending on the situation you face. Second, you can change your mindset if you pay attention and choose growth.

Dweck also acknowledges that mindset can be negatively shaped by those in authority, such as teachers, parents and managers, who might tell you that you are not capable of learning or developing. But whatever others might think, your mindset is your own and you can actively choose to take steps to develop and deploy a growth mindset more frequently.

Here are some things to consider.

Acknowledge your imperfections

Acknowledging and embracing your imperfections and those of others will enable you to see which of your weaknesses you might want to improve – and to understand that everyone is a work in progress.

Face your challenges and help your colleagues to face theirs

If you or somebody in your team feels daunted by a new challenge, try to reframe it positively and look for the inherent opportunity – for example, the opportunity to learn, or to succeed with a challenge in a new area. The key is to step outside your comfort zone, experiment, and discover abilities you didn't know you had.

Stop seeking approval

Trying to measure up to the expectations of others doesn't help to build a growth mindset. Instead, focus on the task, the skills you need, and your own and your team's needs. The approval of others is of limited use and can provide a complicated distraction.

Use feedback constructively and give it thoughtfully

Be open to the suggestions and views of others, recognising that people with a different perspective may be a valuable source of input and guidance.

The Stanford method of giving feedback is a useful tool and a great example of a growth mindset in action. It adopts the "I like, I wish, what if" approach.

For example:

- "I like how passionate you were during this morning's product presentation."
- "I wish you had focused more on the benefits of the product that you know so much about."
- "What if you went through the presentation to check where you could save some time, so you have more time for the Q&A at our next presentation?"

See also chapters 44 and 45 which also address giving feedback.

Value the process as well as the end result

Clearly, results count. However, acknowledging yourself or somebody for trying different strategies to make things happen, consulting others, being bold and creative can all be causes for celebration. Dweck's view is that adopting this way of working may lead to better results next time. Conversely, failing to value the process will make learning, progress (and boldness) much harder to achieve.

"Not yet" is OK

When you or one of your colleagues is struggling with a task, remind yourself that it has not been mastered "yet". If you stick with it, time and practice will lead to improvement.

Thought starters

- Reflect on whether you tend towards more of a fixed or a growth mindset. When is your mindset more fixed?
- How do you try to build on strengths and improve? How well do you list and prioritise your challenges?
- To what extent are you able to reframe effectively, and view challenges as opportunities?
- How often and how well do you step outside your comfort zone?
- How effectively do you give and receive constructive feedback?

What next?

Watch "Developing a growth mindset" by Carol Dweck on YouTube.

5

Psychological safety

Why a safe working environment is the key
to better learning and performance

The big picture

When Google wanted to understand what made its best teams tick, it embarked on a large-scale internal research project – Project Aristotle – designed to answer a simple question: "What makes a team effective at Google?" After some suitably sophisticated data modelling, the results were clear: high performance was less about *who* was on the team, and more about *how* the team worked together. The researchers identified five key factors that improved those team dynamics. Number one on that list, by far the most important, was *psychological safety*. Teams where members felt they would be supported, rather than punished or humiliated, for speaking up, admitting a mistake, asking a question or offering a new idea were more likely to harness the power of diverse ideas, bring in more revenue and generally be more effective.

The concept of psychological safety was introduced in the 1990s by organisational psychologist William Kahn as part of his work on what drives employee engagement. Subsequently, Professor Amy Edmondson of Harvard Business School brought the concept to a global audience with the work that underpins her book *The Fearless Organization*. She defined psychological safety as "the belief that one will not be punished or humiliated for speaking up with ideas, questions, concerns, or mistakes".

The embrace of psychological safety across organisations reflects and responds to the evolving nature of work and the move from rigid hierarchical structures. These days, organisations need to recognise the value of diverse perspectives and input from individuals at all levels. By creating an environment where everyone feels empowered to share ideas and concerns without fear of reprisal or judgement, organisations benefit from the collective intelligence of a wider base. This fosters innovation, trust and collaboration, enabling growth.

About the idea

Amy Edmondson's research suggests that psychological safety is an important predictor of team and individual performance. It is essential for enabling team members to take risks, learn from their mistakes, and innovate. When team members feel safe to speak up and share their ideas, they are more likely to engage in open and honest communication, which can lead to improved decision-making and problem-solving.

High levels of psychological safety enable people to feel secure and able to share ideas, contribute and be themselves. This contrasts with low psychological safety, where people are predominantly concerned about how they and their contributions will be viewed, and are anxious not to make a misstep.

Everyone at work, especially a leader, has a responsibility to help create cultures where psychological safety can flourish. That means being intentional in the following ways.

Encourage open and honest communication

Colleagues should feel comfortable speaking up and sharing their thoughts and ideas, even if these are different from other people's thoughts and ideas. Everyone should feel able to ask for help.

Provide opportunities to voice opinions

Dedicated time should be set aside for team members to share their thoughts and ideas. Everyone should be encouraged to contribute.

Build trust and respect

Trust and respect among team members are essential for creating a positive and supportive work environment. Team members should feel that their colleagues value their opinions and ideas and will treat them with respect, even if they disagree. There should be no sense of one team member undermining another.

Promote a culture of inclusion and belonging

Team members should feel valued and included, regardless of their background, seniority or role. Diverse perspectives and ideas are sought out, welcomed, valued – and acted upon.

Create a safe space for learning and growth

Colleagues should feel comfortable making mistakes and learning from them. Team members are encouraged to take (calculated) risks, to reflect on their work and identify areas for improvement.

The opposite of psychological safety is *psychological danger*. Edmondson talks about the problem of "dangerous silences", where individuals withhold their thoughts, concerns or ideas due to fear or perceived negative consequences; people may worry about being ridiculed, judged or punished. Edmondson's work has looked at the impact of dangerous silences in high-stakes environments, such as complex medical procedures. For example, a nurse notices that a critical step has been missed, but established hierarchies and cultures prevent her from speaking up. The oversight and the nurse's silence have the potential to be life-threatening.

The same principle applies even when the stakes are lower. For example, a team member has reservations about a new project, but chooses to remain silent because she doesn't want to be seen as negative or not a team player. This does not help the team to consider those concerns, which may mean that they miss something that could cause delays or expense and have a big impact.

In practice

Psychological safety is all about creating the right conditions for learning and performance. Building safe workplaces takes practice, intention and skill. Fortunately, Edmondson has developed some useful tools and assessments that can be used to develop your practice. Here are some pointers.

Assess the current level of psychological safety

Start by openly discussing how safe people feel at work – for example, by conducting surveys or focus groups. This can help identify areas for improvement and provide a baseline for tracking progress.

Edmondson has identified seven statements that can be used to frame this process.

1. If you make a mistake on this team, it is often held against you.
2. Members of this team are able to bring up problems and tough issues.
3. People on this team sometimes reject others for being different.
4. It is safe to take a risk in this team.
5. It is difficult to ask other members of this team for help.
6. No one on this team would deliberately act in a way that undermines my efforts.
7. Working with members of this team, my unique skills and talents are valued and used.

Set the stage

Make clear expectations about failure, uncertainty and interdependencies. Be clear about what's at stake, why your work matters, who benefits, and why. The aim is to create shared expectations and meaning.

Invite participation

Be clear that no one has all the answers. Encourage questioning and constructive challenge. Role model active listening. Set up active and intentional structures and routines for discussion and input. Help people to feel confident that their voice is welcome.

For example, you could set aside time at the start or end of regular meetings for team members to share their thoughts and ideas. You may also actively encourage the sharing of diverse perspectives and ideas, such as inviting people from outside your team or group to share their views and experiences on specific issues.

Respond productively: express appreciation

Ask people their opinions and value whatever considered response comes your way. You don't have to agree but you should listen carefully and acknowledge the contribution.

Think about ways in which you can destigmatise failure, looking forward and offering help when things go wrong. The key is to develop cultures of continuous learning.

Thought starters

How psychologically safe do you consider your team and organisation to be?

How could you improve awareness about the importance and power of safe working environments?

Are there sufficient proactive opportunities for people to have their say?

Are you and colleagues willing to take risks and try new things?

Do team members feel comfortable making decisions, or do they worry about potential mistakes?

What next?

Read *The Fearless Organisation: Creating Psychological Safety in the Workplace for Learning, Innovation and Growth* by Amy C. Edmondson.

6

The GROW model of coaching

Making coaching practical, goal-oriented and effective

The big picture

The steady rise of coaching since the 1980s has been driven largely by a desire to deliver immediate and practical benefits, both for the individual being coached and, by extension, their employer. A coaching model developed by the British racing driver, author and pioneer of executive coaching Sir John Whitmore meets this challenge by helping coaches deliver sessions that are practical and effective. The framework helps people to focus on their goals, reality, options and way forward (GROW), as well as their will to do this.

Whereas coaching originally focused on developing top-level managers and leaders – expensive employees deemed worthy of costly one-to-one coaching – people today often see coaching simply as another form of communication and development.

As a result, many organisations have built coaching capability internally. The GROW model has helped to democratise coaching and significantly broadened access to coaching within the workplace, benefiting individuals and organisations alike.

About the idea

Coaching is a goal-oriented, non-directive and learner-led discussion, in which a coach helps an individual to achieve a goal. The coach provides practical *support* by helping the individual explore and focus on the goal, and *challenge* by encouraging the individual to venture into areas they may have disregarded or avoided.

Whitmore's GROW model recognises the support and challenge inherent in effective coaching, and provides a framework for coaching with four stages.

Goals

The coach helps the learner focus and precisely understand their intention and priority, clarifying and understanding the specific outcome that the learner wants to achieve. This can be an *end goal*, such as achieving sales revenues of £1m within a year, or a *performance goal*, such as delivering an engaging presentation or becoming a better public speaker. This provides the practical outcome that the coaching work will support.

Reality

The second stage involves the coach exploring the reality of the learner's situation. This matters because it highlights and prioritises the most significant influences as well as the motivations and benefits of achieving the goal. This stage not only informs the process of progressing the goal, but also helps generate the desire and momentum that may be needed if the goal is particularly difficult or daunting.

Options

In this stage the coach helps the learner explore options, generate ideas, and ultimately choose the best route to achieving their goal. This stage provides the coach with the opportunity to reframe situations that at first appear to be obstacles as something more constructive.

Way forward/wrap-up/will/when

The final stage involves the coach helping the individual to discuss goals, reality and options in a practical, specific and time-constrained action plan. It also involves the coach checking that the individual has the commitment to progressing the goal, and that this commitment to act will last well beyond the coaching sessions.

In practice

The GROW model relies on several fundamental coaching skills, notably active listening and questioning. These include:

- giving and receiving feedback, particularly forward-facing, non-judgemental guidance
- demonstrating a positive regard and intent to help the person being coached
- being objective about the goal being discussed
- evaluating what to do and when to help the person develop and learn
- establishing rapport and being assertive when needed. This enables the coach to provide challenge without it being misconstrued as hostile or judgemental.

Effective coaches accept learners for who they are. They provide encouragement and support, especially after setbacks and mistakes, and they give specific praise.

Coaches also set positive expectations, respect confidentiality and, crucially, help the person being coached to find the answer for themselves. In this way they build confidence as well as developing experience and shaping mindsets.

Remember that coaching is underpinned by questioning that encourages the learner to come up with their own solutions. Suggestions and examples are highlighted below, but it is worth remembering that the best coaches find the style, tone of voice and questions that best suit their context and the individual they are coaching.

Goals

This stage focuses on the individual's aims and priorities and sets the agenda. The outcome is a clear goal for the session.

Questions include:

- What is your goal? What are you trying to achieve?
- What are your priorities?
- How will you know when you have achieved your goal?
- Is the goal specific and measurable?
- What will success look like?

Reality

The coach then explores the individual's current position: the reality of their circumstances and concerns about the goal. The coach needs to help the learner analyse and understand the most relevant issues they face. The coach can also provide information and summarise the situation, helping to clarify the reality.

Questions include:

- Why is this goal significant? Why does it matter?
- What are the major issues you are encountering (or will encounter)?
- Are these issues major or minor? How could their effect be reduced?
- What other issues are there that may affect your goal?
- Can you control the result? What don't you have control over?
- What are the milestones or key points to achieving your goal?
- Who is involved and what effect could they have?

As a result of this discussion, the goal itself may need to be revisited and revised.

Options

At this stage the coach helps the individual to generate options, strategies and action plans for achieving their goal.

Questions include:

- What options do you have?
- Which option do you favour and why?
- If you had unlimited resources, what options would you have?
- What would be the perfect or ideal solution? What would it take to achieve (or partially achieve) this solution?

Way forward/wrap-up/will/when

The final stage of a coaching session can often be rushed, yet it is one of the most significant. The aim is to agree what needs to be done. The coach should be a sounding board, highlighting strengths and weaknesses, testing the planned approach and offering additional perspectives.

Questions include:

- What are you going to do, and when?
- Who needs to know?
- What support and resources do you need, and how will you get them?
- How will you overcome obstacles and ensure success?

Effective plans should incorporate a robust review and feedback process to check progress and provide motivation.

Thought starters

- How ready do you feel to act as a coach?
- How will you develop your skills and effectiveness as a coach?
- How might you apply the GROW model, at the right time and in the right way?

- Which part of the GROW model is the most challenging for you?
- Reflect on whether you would benefit from coaching. What would be your top two or three goals?

What next?

Read *Coaching for Performance: The Principles and Practice of Coaching and Leadership* by John Whitmore.

7

The Myers-Briggs Type Indicator

Understanding individuals and their impact on teams

The big picture

The Myers-Briggs Type Indicator (MBTI®) is the world's most recognised personality assessment and one of the first to become widely used. Developed by Katharine Briggs and her daughter Isabel Briggs Myers in the 1940s, the MBTI is based on the theories of Swiss psychiatrist Carl Jung and draws on his seminal work of 1921, *Psychological Types*.

The MBTI is designed to be accessible, easy to understand and apply, and is used by individuals and organisations worldwide. The assessment is managed and debriefed by qualified practitioners, and the results are often the foundation of interviews, role allocation, team formations and feedback, and can form an important part of personal development plans.

The MBTI can also help individuals understand themselves (and others) better. It can help teams to understand how to maximise their productivity and effectiveness by increasing the quality of interactions between team members.

About the idea

The MBTI is an assessment instrument designed to identify an individual's personality type, strengths, preferences and perception of the world. It also highlights how they interact and ultimately provides insight into how they might make decisions.

The MBTI is not a test – there are no correct or incorrect answers. It is a tool which leads to better self-understanding.

The current version of the MBTI features between 88 and 93 questions (the precise number depends on the region). Each question offers two options from which the respondent must select one. From their answers, an individual is identified as having one of 16 personality types, based on combining preferences across four dimensions.

Introversion (I) – Extraversion (E)

This describes how an individual interacts with the world around them and the individuals within it, showing where people get their focus and energy. Everyone spends time in both areas, depending on the situation and setting, but most people define a greater preference for one area over the other.

Introverts are thought of as "inward-turning". They tend to be more thought-oriented and reserved, getting their energy from reflecting on their own ideas, thoughts and memories, as well as time alone or in small groups.

Extraverts are thought of as "outward turning". They tend to be seen as action-oriented, getting their energy from interacting with people and taking action. Extraverts typically enjoy being the centre of attention, being seen as enthusiastic and assertive.

Sensing (S) – Intuition (N)

This focuses on how an individual gathers information.

Sensing individuals (sensors) prefer specifics such as facts, dates and times. Sensors enjoy experiencing situations, seeking inputs that are real and tangible – they want to know what is happening and base their actions on facts.

Intuitive individuals look for patterns, possibilities and impressions. These people derive information by looking at the big picture, focusing on relationships and connectivity between facts and concepts, and are often more attuned to emerging trends and new opportunities.

Thinking (T) – Feeling (F)

This dimension focuses on how an individual makes decisions.

Thinkers like facts and data, and will look at the logical consequences as a result of a choice or action. They will be energised by examining a situation or challenge, and will typically analyse, evaluate and report before making a recommendation.

Feeling individuals prefer to place themselves in a situation and to consider the impact on other individuals and emotions in their decisions. Feelers are energised by supporting and praising others and seeking harmony.

Judging (J) – Perceiving (P)

This dimension is concerned with how an individual interacts with the world when making decisions.

Individuals with a preference for *judging* prefer structure and definite parameters. They like living and working in a planned and ordered manner, with structure and routine.

Individuals with a preference for *perceiving* prefer flexibility and adaptability, not wanting to be held to a plan or structure. They like to live and work in an open and spontaneous manner, seeking to understand situations and not be constrained by them. These individuals are energised by spontaneity and using their resourcefulness.

At the end of the questionnaire, people emerge with a four-letter descriptor which encapsulates their preferences – for example, INTJ (introversion, intuition, thinking, judging) or ESPF (extroversion, sensing, feeling, perceiving), or any other combination.

The MBTI has endured for decades because of its versatility. For example, it is often used to assess people as part of a hiring process, as well as before training programmes, at the start of coaching assignments, and to assess suitability for new roles and new project teams. In these situations, looking at someone's personality and approach may focus, for example, on when a trait is most pronounced, as well as the consequences, both positive and negative.

However, the MBTI has been called into question by a number of researchers and critics, who challenge its validity on a number of fronts.

- Some studies have found that the MBTI is not a reliable predictor of behaviour and may not accurately reflect people's true personalities.
- It has also been criticised for its deterministic nature, suggesting that people are fixed in their personality types and cannot change. This can be limiting and may not be an accurate portrayal of the way that personalities develop and change over time.
- Questions have also been raised about its reliability. People's scores on the test may vary significantly when they take it multiple times, and the outcome is solely dependent on an individual answering honestly. This lack of reliability raises questions about the validity of the test and its ability to measure personality accurately.
- Critics also argue that the MBTI's 16 personality types are too narrow, and do not capture the complexity and nuance of human personality and different cultural contexts.

There is, of course, an element of truth in all these challenges. A crucial counter is to remember that the MBTI is firmly focused on people's *preferences*, not hard and fast traits. For example, you may have a preference towards introversion, but you can still exhibit extrovert behaviours (like leading a meeting or giving a presentation) when needed; you might just need to spend more time alone to prepare and then recover afterwards.

MBTI insights are never a silver bullet. They need to be considered alongside other factors and considerations when people are being assessed or are assessing themselves.

In practice

The Myers-Briggs Type Indicator is typically administered by certified MBTI practitioners, and there are different reports available with varying levels of insights which can be applied to individuals and teams.

The four dimensions combine to create 16 distinct MBTI personality types, identified by a four-letter acronym, each with pros and cons.

TABLE 1: THE MBTI PERSONALITY TYPES

INFP

· Creative with a strong moral compass, they look to make the world a better place.	· May struggle to speak up in meetings and risk being overlooked.

ISFP

· Easy-going and cooperative, they tend to be reserved and artistic.	· Being assertive and making difficult decisions could be challenging, leading to less influence in the workplace.

ESFP

· Adaptable, spontaneous and outgoing, they enjoy being with people and taking centre stage.	· May find it difficult to meet deadlines and finish what they started.

ESTP

· Inventive and practical, they bring others along with their energy, finding solutions with others.	· May not be effective at managing time or long complex problems.

ISTP

· Independent and patient, they remain calm and make effective decisions fast.	· May find it hard to see the bigger picture and follow through on projects.

INTP

· Strategic and conceptual, they are able to analyse the world and uncover innovative solutions.	· Working with others and remembering important facts may be difficult.

ENTP

· Inventive and creative, they see connections and concepts within a system, finding new solutions.	· Decision-making may be difficult, and they can be seen as challenging to work with.

ENFP

- Energetic and charismatic, they move quickly between projects considering multiple possibilities and bringing others along.
- May find it hard to prioritise and follow through to complete projects.

INFJ

- Inspirational and creative, they look for a common shared vision.
- May not be seen as individualistic.

ISFJ

- Patient and loyal, they use common sense to solve problems, while protecting their colleagues.
- May be seen as lacking assertiveness.

ESFJ

- Appreciative and outgoing, they see the best in people and enjoy establishing a collaborative approach.
- May find decisions a challenge because they can be overly accepting of others' points of views and needs.

ENFJ

- Inclusive and collaborative, they bring everyone together and represent views.
- May struggle with conflict and lack of consensus, delaying decisions to bring all points of view into account.

ISTJ

- Systematic and dependable, they are task oriented and enjoy working within defined processes and systems.
- May be seen as rigid and inflexible to change and the need of others.

INTJ

- Creative and innovative, they can look at complex problems with a long-term innovative view.
- Can often be viewed as impersonal and unappreciative of others' input or points of view.

ENTJ

- Confident and strategic, they organise and bring others along to complete long-term projects.
- May overlook the contribution of colleagues.

ESTJ

- Assertive and driven, they are goal oriented, making tough decisions when needed. They will use an extensive network of contacts to reach project conclusions.
- May find it challenging to consider the feelings of others and build rapport under stress.

Knowing your preferences and those of others can be invaluable when developing self-awareness and relationships. In a new project team, for example, people who are not used to working together may be better able to realise where their contributions should focus, as well as recognising the value and contributions of others.

Like similar diagnostics, the MBTI has its uses if employed with care and finesse. Just don't expect it to solve all your problems.

Thought starters

- How much do you know about your own strengths and weaknesses and those of your colleagues, particularly in a team context?
- How could the MBTI help you and your colleagues become more effective?
- How could you use the MBTI tool to gain a better understanding of your team and how to lead them?
- What MBTI personality types would benefit your team or organisation to achieve its goals?
- How could you use the MBTI to develop yourself?

What next?

Check out the resources at the Myers-Briggs Company website: www.themyersbriggs.com

8

Luft and Ingham's Johari window

Recognising personal blind spots and increasing self-awareness

The big picture

Everyone has blind spots: aspects of themselves – traits, values, actions and behaviours – that they're not fully conscious of. It might be obvious to others, for example, that consistently turning up late for meetings is annoying but it never crosses your mind that it might be a problem. Or perhaps you can see that others are dominating (or withdrawing) in meetings, without wondering if you might be doing the same.

Some of the hardest blind spots are those originating from a positive intent. You may think you are trying to help, but there is a huge risk that your tone or approach will be patronising or annoying without you being remotely aware that this is how your good intentions are being received. The truth is that everyone has blind spots; they can be irritating at best and downright damaging at worst. Boosting your self-awareness is essential, and needs to be worked at constantly; as you and your circumstances change, so will your blind spots.

That's why tools that can help us to improve our self-awareness and see ourselves as others see us are so valuable. The Johari window was created in 1955 by psychologists Joseph Luft and Harrington Ingham (hence the name Jo-Hari) to do just that: to help people understand their relationship with themselves and with others.

The model built on techniques such as the Myers-Briggs Type Indicator (see Chapter 7) and, like the MBTI, was among the first tools to introduce rigorous psychological techniques into the workplace. It did this by shining a light on the need for people to be self-aware, open and continually learning, a challenge that is now commonplace and a widely recognised part of being an effective contributor at work.

About the idea

The Johari window is a visual model that is typically used to develop self-awareness, as a personal development tool, and to build better workplace relationships.

There are two central ideas behind the Johari window. First, you can boost your trustworthiness by disclosing information about yourself; openness and authenticity, therefore, are vital. Second, receiving feedback and support from others is a valuable way to learn about yourself, resolve personal issues and develop the way you work.

The Johari window has four panes or "quadrants", each one containing information about an individual's self-awareness and how they are perceived by others, as Figure 1 shows.

Figure 1: **The four quadrants of the Johari window**

	Known to me	Not known to me
Known to others	Open Things I know and like others to know	Blind spots Things others know but I do not
Not known to others	Hidden Things I know but conceal from others	Unknown Things neither I nor others know

The outer lines of the model represent the whole person and the quadrants can enlarge or reduce in size depending on the answers given. For example, a person with only a few hidden, blind spots and unknowns is likely to be a very open individual, which can be represented by increasing the size of that quadrant accordingly. The model helps to develop self-awareness by clarifying what an individual knows about themselves, and uncovering how they appear to others.

Here's what the quadrants represent.

Open: known to me and known to others

These are the things that you know and others know about you too. This is how you project yourself and how you like others to regard you.

Individuals who are self-aware and are understood by those around them will have a large open area. Conversely, people who lack self-awareness will have a small open area.

Blind spots: not known to me but known to others

These are things others know about you, but you do not. These are characteristics and behaviours that you are unaware of but that others see and experience, like the negative impact of consistently turning up late for meetings. Knowing how you appear to others is essential to improving self-awareness. Blind spots in teams can cause friction and resentment.

A large blind area may mean that you are unaware of the impact of your behaviour on others or may be in denial. It may also mean that people are keeping what they know about you to themselves.

Hidden: known to me but not known to others

This is a façade, the hidden self: things that you know about yourself but conceal from others. Being aware of these traits (and the reasons for concealing them) heightens self-awareness and helps to build trust and strengthen relationships.

You need to consider whether your hidden traits are affecting your work or the work of those around you. No one has to reveal everything about themselves at work. But when hidden traits remain hidden for no real reason, they can lead to mistrust, confusion and isolation.

Unknown: not known to me and not known to others

This quadrant focuses on the unknown self: things that neither you nor others know. A large unknown area may result from inexperience or an ability of which you are unaware. This requires you to look reflectively at yourself and with others close to you, to reveal your deeper motivations, beliefs and issues.

In practice

Self-disclosure

To use the Johari window, identify your personal characteristics by choosing from the 56 adjectives of the Johari window list that best describe you. You can either use these, or develop your own. The adjectives are shown in Table 2.

TABLE 2: THE 56 ADJECTIVES USED TO APPLY TO THE JOHARI QUADRANTS

Able	Energetic	Loving	Searching
Accepting	Extroverted	Mature	Self-assertive
Adaptable	Friendly	Modest	Self-conscious
Bold	Giving	Nervous	Sensible
Brave	Happy	Observant	Sentimental
Calm	Helpful	Organised	Shy
Caring	Idealistic	Patient	Silly
Cheerful	Independent	Powerful	Spontaneous
Clever	Ingenious	Proud	Sympathetic
Complex	Intelligent	Quiet	Tense
Confident	Introverted	Reflective	Trustworthy
Dependable	Kind	Relaxed	Warm
Dignified	Knowledgeable	Religious	Wise
Empathetic	Logical	Responsive	Witty

Feedback

The next step is to ask one or more of your colleagues for feedback. From that list of 56 adjectives, ask them to choose all those that they feel describe you.

Organise your personal insights

Next, draw a Johari window and complete each of the quadrants.

- The open area should include the adjectives that both you and your colleagues chose to describe you.
- The hidden area includes adjectives that only you chose to describe yourself.
- The blind area contains only those adjectives selected by your colleagues to describe you.
- The unknown area has adjectives that were not chosen by you or your colleagues but could be feasible as your self-awareness increases.

Review the Johari window and set clear goals

Review the Johari window you have created. The aim is to expand the size of the open area and reduce the size of the other quadrants. Additional feedback and further discussion may be valuable, and personal coaching may help too.

Bear in mind that the results may vary depending on who you involve and how well they know you. For that reason, a variety of inputs is useful. Honest feedback and personal disclosure are essential, and you need to be receptive to the feedback you receive. Self-disclosure expands the open area vertically; sensitive feedback from others expands it horizontally.

The aim is to reduce the traits that we hide from others, and become aware of traits we're blind to, as a way of increasing self-awareness and, potentially, building stronger and more effective relationships.

Thought starters

- How do you think completing a Johari window exercise might support your personal development?
- Think about some trusted colleagues you could ask for feedback.

- Think about any traits you're concealing from others. Why are you hiding them?
- Would your relationships benefit from greater openness?
- How can you help others to develop their self-awareness?
- How can you challenge yourself, pushing yourself out of your comfort zone? What new activities or experiences would help develop your expertise, experience and self-confidence?

What next?

Read *Self-Awareness* in the HBR "Emotional Intelligence" series by Daniel Goleman, Robert Steven Kaplan, Susan David and Tasha Eurich.

9

Csikszentmihalyi's *Flow*

Understanding excellence

The big picture

Remember the last time you witnessed an incredible athlete or an amazing team, a group of brilliant musicians, or perhaps a dance troupe that seemed to express perfection. What you witnessed was almost certainly Mihaly Csikszentmihalyi's concept of *flow*. Many factors contribute to great performances and success – such as creativity, physicality, timing and context – but flow is invariably present too.

Csikszentmihalyi, a Hungarian-American psychologist, introduced his concept of flow in the 1970s. The term refers to a state of complete absorption and engagement in an activity, where an individual is completely focused on what they are doing. The concept has become hugely influential in a wide variety of fields, including psychology and business as well as in sports, music and the performing arts.

The concept of flow was developed through extensive qualitative and quantitative research. During the process, Csikszentmihalyi used the word "autotelic" to describe activities that are intrinsically rewarding and satisfying. Experiencing flow leads to a state of "optimal experience" where the increased satisfaction, creativity and overall well-being result in enhanced engagement, performance and outcomes.

About the idea

Csikszentmihalyi's flow centres around the concept of optimal experience and the conditions that lead to an individual's peak performance, satisfaction and fulfilment.

The fundamental aspects of flow are as follows.

Focusing attention

In a state of flow, individuals experience intense concentration and focus attention on the task at hand. The mind becomes fully engaged and distractions fade away.

Losing self-consciousness

Flow involves a diminishing awareness of self and ego. The distinction between the individual and the activity blurs, resulting in a sense of oneness with the task.

Clear goals and feedback

People are more likely to achieve a state of flow if they have clear goals and immediate feedback. They know what needs to be done, and receiving effective feedback on their progress allows them to make necessary adjustments along the way.

Balancing challenge and skill

Flow occurs when the level of challenge in an activity matches the individual's skill level. If the task is too easy it can lead to boredom; if it's too difficult it may cause anxiety. Flow is found in the optimal balance between challenge and skill.

Feeling control

Flow is associated with a feeling of control over one's own actions. People feel competent and capable, with a sense that their skills are meeting the demands of the task effectively. This leads to satisfaction and other valuable emotions, such as confidence.

Distorting time

People in a state of flow often experience the perception that time is being distorted. Hours may feel like minutes as people are fully engrossed in the activity.

Intrinsic motivation and enjoyment

Flow is typically associated with intrinsic motivation, where people engage in an activity for the sheer joy of the experience rather than external rewards. The activity itself becomes rewarding and even pleasurable.

Acting effortlessly

Flow involves a sense of effortlessness in performing the activity. Despite the challenges, people feel a natural and smooth progression in their actions.

Merging action and awareness

Flow is characterised by a merging of action and awareness. Individuals are fully present in the moment, and their actions align seamlessly with their intentions.

An autotelic experience

The presence of flow is considered highly autotelic – that is, intrinsically rewarding and satisfying – because the activity itself is fulfilling.

Breaking down the psychological components of great work and strong performance supports many of the activities we take part in at work, from setting objectives and clear goals to giving feedback and developing capability. If you feel confident, capable, utterly absorbed in your work and, ultimately, fulfilled and successful, then it is likely you are mastering the concept of flow.

In practice

Csikszentmihalyi's concept of flow has been applied in various practical contexts to enhance individual and collective experiences and performance. In the workplace, achieving a state of flow can be achieved in ways that provide significant personal benefits, improving effectiveness and career success.

There are several things you can do to develop and benefit from a state of flow.

Develop your focus

This can be achieved by setting yourself the right goals (see Chapter 39), as well as removing distractions and interruptions.

Build self-confidence

This may involve building up to the task gradually over time, in incremental steps, practising and, crucially, receiving feedback. Remember that feedback is one of the three conditions that need to be present to develop a state of flow (the others being goals and balance).

Strengthen your skills

Often we focus on bringing underperforming skills up to an acceptable level. However, to develop a sense of flow it can also help to work on moving from good to great: in other words, developing your existing expertise and skill so that they become truly exceptional.

Stretch and challenge yourself

What more could you do to extend your capabilities by developing new skills? Taking control of your own development brings with it a sense of agency that is important for confidence and flow.

Understand your motivations

Not every task gives us a feeling of flow. The key lies in understanding which tasks feel more routine or mundane to you and which ones excite and drive you.

The practical application of flow highlights its versatility in improving aspects of human experience and interactions, from learning and work to creativity and well-being.

Thought starters

- What were you doing the last time you were completely absorbed in an activity?
- What can you do to adopt some of the principles of flow for yourself and your colleagues?
- What role can feedback play in creating optimal learning conditions?
- What everyday activities align with flow? How can you improve the way you complete these activities?
- How can you describe and share the ideas behind flow and how it could benefit your colleagues and clients?

What next?

Read *Flow: The Psychology of Happiness* by Mihaly Csikszentmihalyi.

10

VUCA: volatility, uncertainty, complexity and ambiguity

Navigating a world of challenge and change

The big picture

First used in 1987, the acronym VUCA stands for volatility, uncertainty, complexity and ambiguity, and draws on the leadership theories of Warren Bennis and Burt Nanus, American academics, authors and pioneers in leadership development theory. Introduced by the US Army War College, VUCA was subsequently used extensively by the military to describe and understand a post-Cold War world.

These days, the term VUCA is often used more generally to describe geopolitical and business environments that are characterised by a high degree of change and unpredictability.

Bennis and Nanus argue that to succeed in a VUCA environment, organisations must be adaptable and agile, with a strong and clear sense of strategy and vision. They also emphasise the importance of building strong relationships and fostering a culture of innovation and continuous learning.

About the idea

The VUCA framework provides a way to understand and navigate a complex and constantly changing business environment. It highlights the importance of being prepared for situations that can be defined and framed as being unpredictable, by addressing the qualities of volatility, uncertainty, complexity and ambiguity.

Volatility is the rapid and unexpected changes that organisations face. These include economic, political, social and technological changes.

Uncertainty is the inability to predict the future. This unpredictability can include events such as natural disasters, market fluctuations, and changes in consumer behaviour or fashion.

Complexity is the intricate nature of the business environment. This can include the number of stakeholders involved, the number of variables at play, and the interdependent nature of business processes.

Ambiguity is the lack of clarity or certainty in business. This can include the lack of clear goals, conflicting information and the difficulty of making informed decisions.

By identifying and understanding the elements of the VUCA framework, you can gain a deeper understanding of the challenges and opportunities of a complex and changing landscape. That understanding can enhance strategic planning and enable you to develop more flexible and adaptable strategies equipped to handle rapid changes and unexpected events.

There are several approaches and alternatives to VUCA that are often used in a similar way. These include:

- *CHAOS:* used to describe a situation that is complex, high-impact, ambiguous and dynamic.

- *FOCUS*: used to describe a situation that is fragile, oppressive, complex, unpredictable and stressful. It is similar to VUCA, but emphasises the negative aspects of operating in a complex and uncertain environment.

- *VUCA Prime*: another term coined by the US Army War College. Similar to VUCA, it adds an additional "P" for "possibility", intended to emphasise the opportunities that can arise in a volatile, uncertain, complex and ambiguous environment.

- *VUCA 2.0*: builds on VUCA Prime by adding two more elements – innovation and resilience. It encourages organisations to embrace change and adaptability to thrive in a complex and uncertain world.

In practice

The essence of a VUCA framework is the ability to recognise and navigate challenges and opportunities to foster adaptability, resilience and effective personal and organisational leadership. It emphasises the importance of understanding and embracing a dynamic situation to be successful and grow.

To use the VUCA framework on the ground, try these steps.

Identify the elements of VUCA that are relevant

Conduct a VUCA analysis, running through each of the letters of the acronym to identify the potential challenges and opportunities you face, including economic, political, social, environmental and technological changes.

Develop strategies to respond to VUCA

Based on the relevance and impact of the elements of VUCA you identified, you can then develop strategies to respond. Build flexibility and adaptability into planning processes and decision-making structures, as well as developing contingency plans.

Encourage a culture of innovation and learning

To be agile and adaptable in a VUCA environment, you need to be open to new ideas and willing to learn and adapt. Provide opportunities for yourself and others to learn and grow and encourage a culture of innovation and experimentation.

Build relationships

Build strong relationships, notably with customers, employees, suppliers and partners. Regular communication and collaboration are key, together with a focus on building trust and mutual understanding.

Provide strong leadership and a clear vision

Strong leadership throughout organisations with a clear, guiding vision that is well communicated and understood is crucial to sustain an organisation in difficult times. A clear direction will inspire others and encourage people to build resilience in the face of uncertainty.

The late Steve Jobs provides a classic example of being able to exploit the opportunities inherent in a VUCA environment. Under his leadership, Apple consistently demonstrated strong leadership and a clear vision. Jobs had a relentless focus on innovation, design excellence and creating user-friendly products. This clear vision helped Apple navigate multiple VUCA challenges, such as changing customer demographics and preferences, intense competition, litigation, supply chain challenges and disruptive technological advances.

Thought starters

- Volatility: how can you improve your response to unexpected challenges or opportunities that arise?
- Uncertainty: how do you approach decision-making when faced with limited information or unpredictable outcomes?
- Complexity: how do you manage multiple responsibilities or conflicting priorities?
- Ambiguity: how do you deal with ambiguity and make decisions in complex, uncertain and volatile situations?
- How can you build greater resilience, and the ability to come through challenging times in your professional life?

What next?

Read *Leaders: Strategies for Taking Charge* by Warren Bennis and Burt Nanus.

11

Black swans

Expecting the unexpected

The big picture

A black swan event is an outlier – an event that is rare, unpredicted and beyond the realms of normal, conventional expectations. Black swan events have a big impact, but they can, in retrospect, be explained and rationalised. They have shaped the modern world in all sorts of ways, whether through developments in technology and science or changes to business, education, culture and politics. As the world becomes increasingly connected, black swans are becoming more consequential.

Human nature and our brains are conditioned to create explanations for events after the fact, which are then nuanced to make them appear to have been less random, more predictable and easier to explain. This *hindsight bias* creates blind spots, with the result that people may not learn from their mistakes.

Nassim Nicholas Taleb, a philosopher, essayist and former options trader, wrote *The Black Swan: The Theory of the Highly Improbable* in 2007. He suggested that there are industries more prone to hindsight bias, and that the human brain can be retrained to recognise black swan events and overcome ingrained cognitive bias.

About the idea

Until the late 17th century, people in the "Old World" (meaning Europe and the Middle East), Taleb declares, believed that all swans were white, solely because no one had seen a swan of any other colour. That was until Dutch explorer Willem de Vlamingh arrived in Australia in 1697 and saw the black-feathered variety. Since then, black swans have become ordinary and commonplace. This is the origin of the concept for Taleb's black swan theory: events that appear impossible or unlikely when they have not yet been seen can later become normal. The human brain assimilates explanations and normalises them.

Some examples of black swan events include the following.

- *The September 11th attacks.* The terrorist attacks on the World Trade Center and the Pentagon were highly unlikely and had a major impact on global politics and security.
- *The global financial crisis of 2008.* The collapse of a previously buoyant housing market and the subsequent financial crisis were unexpected and had far-reaching consequences for the global economy.

Other examples of black swan events include natural disasters, technological disruptions and political upheavals. These events are often characterised by their rarity and their significant impact on society.

Policy analyst Michele Wucker introduced a similar colour-based animal idea in her 2016 book *The Gray Rhino.* Like a black swan, a grey rhino is a high-impact event that is unlikely to occur but has the potential to cause significant damage. However, unlike a black swan event, which is completely unexpected, a grey rhino event is a more visible threat that is often ignored or downplayed.

Wucker argues that grey rhino events are more common and more dangerous than black swans, as they are often ignored or dismissed until it is too late to act. However, they still have the potential to cause significant harm if not properly addressed.

The jury is out over whether the covid-19 pandemic was a black swan or a grey rhino. It may seem to be a black swan in terms of its rapid spread, global impact and magnitude, but the fact that numerous experts and public health organisations were anticipating the risk of a global pandemic might place it in the grey rhino category. There were clear warnings about the potential for a novel virus outbreak and the need for preparedness measures. Therefore, although the specific virus and timing may have been uncertain, the general risk of a pandemic was a visible and known risk that was neglected or not fully addressed by many governments and organisations.

In practice

Taleb's black swan theory claims that rare and unpredictable events have a profound impact on our history and understanding of risk. These events are most often explained retrospectively as if they were predictable, leading societies to underestimate the potential consequences and the need for deeper understanding when looking ahead.

To understand and come through black swan or grey rhino events, you must retrain your thinking. There are several key lessons that can be learned from black swan events.

Do not rely too heavily on historical data

Black swans and grey rhinos tend to fall outside the realm of normal expectations and are difficult to predict based on historical data. It is important to be thoughtful in your predictions and to be aware of the limitations of historical data.

Be prepared for the unexpected

Black swans and grey rhinos are both examples of high-impact, low-probability events that can have significant consequences if not properly anticipated and addressed. It is important to be prepared for the unexpected and to have plans in place to deal with unforeseen events.

Be proactive in addressing potential risk

Grey rhinos are more visible threats that are often ignored or downplayed until it is too late to act. You need to identify and address potential risks rather than ignoring or downplaying them until they become a major problem. Techniques like scenario planning can help you to anticipate and plan.

Be humble in your understanding of the world

Both black swans and grey rhinos serve as reminders of the limitations of human understanding of the world and the role of randomness and uncertainty in shaping events. The concept of black swan events reminds us to be open, curious and humble in understanding the world, and always to be ready for the unexpected.

Thought starters

- Can you think of examples from your career that fit the definition of a black swan or grey rhino event? What were the implications and effects?
- Consider how the black swan concept might challenge traditional notions of risk and probability.
- Can you apply lessons and insights from these theories to your personal decision-making and approach to risk management?
- How can you and your organisation better prepare for, or mitigate, the impact of black swan and grey rhino events?

What next?

Read *The Black Swan: The Impact of the Highly Improbable* by Nassim Nicholas Taleb and *The Gray Rhino: How to Recognise and Act on the Obvious Dangers We Ignore* by Michele Wucker.

12

Scenario planning

Rehearsing the future

The big picture

In the 1960s, oil giant Royal Dutch Shell had a secret weapon. Its head of group planning, Pierre Wack, was a pioneer of the idea of scenario planning, rehearsing different scenarios for the forces likely to affect Shell's future. In 1973, Wack's scenarios became a reality. The 1973 Israeli-Arab war had a dramatic impact on oil companies, with prices increasing fivefold as the Organisation of the Petroleum Exporting Countries (OPEC) began limiting the supply of oil. Fortunately for Shell, Wack's work ensured that the company was prepared for such a change and had already planned a response. When the oil shocks happened, Shell was ahead of its competitors, maximising profits that year and moving from seventh to second place in the table of oil companies' profitability.

Scenarios have remained a vital part of Shell's approach to business strategy ever since, helping the company to understand changes in the business environment, identify new opportunities, explore strategic responses and take long-term decisions.

Scenario planning is not just for large multinational companies, though. It can help organisations of all sizes – and the people who work in them – understand the potential impact of forces that are shaping the future, challenging assumptions and helping them to overcome complacency and "business-as-usual" thinking. Scenarios help people to rehearse the future, allowing them to visualise their responses and their roles in advance.

About the idea

Scenarios inform and guide an organisation's understanding of possible futures that lie ahead and the forces contributing to those events. The outcomes of different responses and their impact can be tested, without risk, by exploring different scenarios. The objective is not to predict the future; it is to visualise events before they happen and explore the options available in response.

Scenario thinking enables people at work to:

- reveal new perspectives and identify gaps in organisational knowledge
- challenge assumptions, overcoming biases and business-as-usual thinking
- understand the present and identify potential trends and issues affecting the business
- encourage people to share information and ideas
- improve responses to events
- promote a shift in attitude and boost resilience in the face of uncertainty
- promote a shared purpose and direction.

Although scenario thinking increased in prominence from the 1970s to the early 2000s, it has since declined in popularity. At least part of the reason for this is the proliferation of random, devastating and largely "unknowable" black swan global events that have shaken organisations in the 21st century (see Chapter 11). Even so, understanding the forces shaping the future of your industry remains a valuable activity and skill, and thinking in terms of scenarios is one of the best ways to do this.

In practice

If you think some scenario planning might be a useful activity for you and your colleagues, here are some ideas for putting it into practice.

Initial planning

The first step is to create a small cross-functional and diverse team known for their innovative and challenging thinking. This team needs to identify gaps in knowledge as well as vulnerabilities, and then work together to create a "history of the future" – a view of what could happen and how it might happen.

These views should be collated, with the main issues, ideas, forces and uncertainties shared and explained. This will help inform the scenarios.

Develop the scenarios

The next step is to understand and explore the forces shaping the future. Work together to develop scenarios that create and assess possible events and their consequences. To do this, take the following steps.

1. Identify the forces that could affect a situation.
2. Agree two possible opposite outcomes (and the forces involved).
3. Identify how these forces are linked.
4. Decide whether each force has a low or high impact and a low or high probability of occurring.
5. Develop likely "histories" that lead to each outcome, detailing the factors involved.

Scenario planning usually results in three potential futures: one with change that is familiar, one with quite profound change, and one that fundamentally reshapes the industry or business.

Analysing and using the scenarios

The final stage focuses on identifying the priorities and concerns of those key actors in the scenario who are outside the organisation, including their likely reactions at different stages.

Then, working backwards from the scenario's future, develop an action plan that brings us back to the present. The idea is that this will help to identify the early signs of change, which means that they can be swiftly and effectively acted upon and help influence an organisation's policies and strategic direction.

Farming provides an interesting example of scenario planning at work, with farmers using scenarios to plan their response depending on whether the harvest will be good or bad. This helps them forecast their sales and their future investments.

Thought starters

- Is your organisation prepared for "what if?" scenarios?
- Who would you involve in scenario planning? Consider people who are not afraid to challenge the status quo as well as having a broad range of experience and expertise.
- How do you and your organisation continue to learn about your industry, the market, customer needs and any emerging trends? Do you consider multiple options – different ways that events may play out – before making big decisions?
- Is your organisation afraid of uncertainty, or do people see it as a potential opportunity?

What next?

Read *Scenarios: The Art of Strategic Conversation* by Kees van der Heijden.

13

Ambidexterity

Balancing the present and future

The big picture

The ability to balance present-day efficiency and future-focused innovation – a concept known as ambidexterity – has become a critical competency for forward-facing and resilient organisations and the people who work in them.

Ambidexterity is the art of achieving stability, efficiency and results today – *exploiting* the current business model and situation – while simultaneously innovating and taking risks that will shape the future: *exploring* options for sustained future success. It signifies the simultaneous need to explore new opportunities and to exploit existing resources.

The concept of an ambidextrous organisation was originally proposed by researcher Robert Duncan in 1976, and at the time was seen through the lens of business strategy and innovation. Charles O'Reilly and Michael Tushman developed the idea further, this time from an organisational learning perspective, encouraging individuals to become ambidextrous too.

In 2000 Mehrdad Baghai, Steven Coley and David White published *The Alchemy of Growth*, which included the model widely known as the McKinsey three horizons model. Their approach provided a blueprint for innovation strategy by encouraging organisations to operate with an eye on three distinct timeframes and activities: making continuous improvements in the immediate short term (horizon 1); extending and expanding the business model in horizon 2; and creating new capabilities and business in horizon 3.

These days, the concept of ambidexterity is used to describe both people and organisations who can navigate complex, changing environments and shift between different modes of operation as needed. Crucially, people are able both to foster creativity and innovation, while also ensuring that the organisation achieves its current core goals and objectives in a timely and efficient manner.

About the idea

Ambidexterity requires people and organisations to focus simultaneously on the present and the future: described as "exploitation" and "exploration".

Exploitation involves making the most of existing resources and capabilities to achieve specific goals. It is important for organisations to exploit their existing resources and capabilities to achieve stability and efficiency.

Exploration involves seeking out new ideas, approaches and opportunities, and is more typically associated with innovation and risk-taking. It is important for organisations to explore new ideas and approaches to stay competitive and adapt to changing market conditions.

There are several key elements of ambidextrous individuals and organisations.

A clear, overarching purpose, vision and identity

A compelling identity for the organisation is a valuable touchstone: it provides constancy and guides the organisation towards its goals and objectives. Crucially, it can allow for competing strategies to be pursued by different business units as long as they reinforce the identity (brand) and help pursue the vision.

Adaptability and agility

The ability to navigate complex and rapidly changing environments and to shift between different modes of operation as needed is essential.

Communication and interpersonal skills

People must be able to communicate and collaborate easily with colleagues and stakeholders in an atmosphere of trust and mutual support.

Informed and balanced decision-making

Decision-making needs to take into account both short-term and long-term goals.

Risk-taking

Creativity and innovation within the organisation must be encouraged, as well as a readiness to learn from mistakes or misfires and the skills to manage and mitigate risk.

Managing exploration and exploitation simultaneously can be complex; it's a challenging task requiring significant skill. Fostering innovation and creativity can also be time consuming and resource intensive, which can be particularly difficult during tough, recessionary times. There is the danger that some people may resist changes to the way that the organisation operates or disagrees with the exploration of new ideas.

But it's clear that, to survive and thrive, organisations need to be able to look to the future as well as the present. This characterises not just ambidextrous leadership but ambidextrous organisations too.

In practice

Ambidexterity is about managing and balancing two seemingly contradictory sets of activities: exploration and exploitation. In practice, here are some things to consider.

Develop a coherent, consistent identity and vision

This needs to connect the organisation's present with its future, showing what needs to be done now, and where that action will lead.

When Jeff Bezos founded Amazon, he was determined that his fledgling enterprise would become a major player in the emerging world of online retail. His actions – for example, reinvesting profits in technology – did not just help the company succeed at the time; they also built huge barriers that future competitors would need to overcome. While building its online retail business, Amazon also invested in branding, data centres and computer algorithms to understand customer preferences and buying habits and in building a range of third-party services. This approach defied the orthodoxy of the early 2000s which expected "tech" businesses to pay large and regular dividends to their shareholders, rather than determinedly reinvesting for the future. Amazon's approach paid off, ensuring a pre-eminent position among global retailers.

A clear vision for the organisation's present and future trajectory guides people's actions and focuses their talents, as well as bringing stakeholders, employees and the wider organisation into play.

Innovate and adapt

It is important to encourage creativity and risk-taking, creating a "no blame" environment where new ideas and approaches are encouraged and can be explored – in other words, psychological safety (see Chapter 5).

Like the McKinsey three horizons model, O'Reilly and Tushman identify three types of innovation that underpin ambidexterity and all need to be in play at the same time.

1. *Incremental innovations*: regular improvements to existing products and operations to boost efficiency and value – for example, adding new features to a successful product or service to boost its appeal and extend its life cycle (see Chapter 29).

2. *Architectural innovations*: applying technological or process advances to change more fundamentally how business operates – for example, the shift from physical to online retailing.

3. *Discontinuous innovations*: radical advances that profoundly alter the basis for competition in an industry, often rendering old products or ways of working obsolete – for example, the rise of digital photography.

Consider how best to support ambidexterity

Depending on your context, you might want to consider how best to manage a more ambidextrous approach to your work. Some organisations have created specialist units to focus on the longer-term innovation horizon, although this can bring with it the danger of creating silos – and does not help to spread longer-term thinking more widely. Others might choose to partner with or use external organisations and resources to boost elements of their exploitation and exploration. Apple, with its extensive network of hardware suppliers and ecosystem of developers, has shown how well this can work.

Smaller teams and individuals might focus on developing a more ambidextrous mindset when developing and implementing strategy.

Make sure that decisions are consistent and informed

This means taking into account both short-term and long-term goals when making decisions and the need for both exploration (of future opportunities) and exploitation (of the current business model and approach).

Thought starters

- Does your organisation have a clear vision and purpose, and an overarching identity that is understood by everyone?
- How can you develop or sustain a culture of innovation and creativity within your team or organisation?
- Are there changes in the market that require you and your colleagues to adapt and evolve? If so, how will you do this?

- How can you encourage risk-taking in some areas, while also ensuring efficiency and stability in others?
- What more can you do to improve openness, trust and teamworking with your colleagues?

What next?

Read the article "The ambidextrous organization" by Charles A. O'Reilly and Michael L. Tushman.

14

Kotter's eight steps for leading change

Adapting in fast-changing times

The big picture

Change seems to be a constant at work today. Whether you're leading, managing or on the receiving end, the pace of change and its often open-ended nature can be difficult to manage, navigate or simply come to terms with. Whether you see change as exciting and full of opportunities or tend to shy away from the unknown, understanding how thinkers have traditionally explored change and how to manage it can help you get to grips with what it means and how to make the most of it.

In the mid-1990s Harvard Business School professor John Kotter studied 100 companies that were going through transitions. He analysed the reasons for their success alongside the pitfalls they encountered, identifying a series of commonly made mistakes which led companies to fail in their ability to transition. Kotter's 1996 book *Leading Change* provided a ground-breaking, practical guide to the challenge of leading people and organisations through times of uncertainty, opportunity and growth.

At the time, economic development was being driven by globalisation, geopolitics (notably the end of the Cold War and the emergence of major new markets in eastern Europe and Asia), deregulation and the rise of new technologies. Kotter highlighted the central point that the way people think about work requires an ability to change, develop and evolve in line with changing times and, ideally, to lead the change and shape the future, rather than being a passive observer and reacting too late.

The ability to understand this new approach to leading change came to be seen as a crucial skill designed to anticipate and provide new opportunities that contrasted with the potentially terminal risks of inaction.

About the idea

Kotter found that successful change was a process rather than an event. This led him to compile his "eight steps for leading change": a sequence of actions to ensure that organisations would succeed in achieving their goals during times of change. Crucially, Kotter highlighted the need for people to pay attention to each of the eight steps if they want to avoid problems and significantly change their organisation.

The eight steps are:

Creating the climate for change

1. Establish a sense of urgency.
2. Form a strong guiding coalition.
3. Create a vision.

Engaging and enabling the organisation

4. Communicate the vision.
5. Empower people to act in line with the vision.
6. Create short-term wins.

Implementing and sustaining the change

7. Consolidate improvements and maintain momentum.
8. Institutionalise the new approaches.

Kotter emphasised that leading people through times of change is about being flexible and practical, shifting the way people think, overcoming obstacles and achieving results that benefit the organisation.

These days, Kotter's approach may seem out of step in a world of work where change is not always a programme or process with defined outcomes that can be planned, or a journey on which people can choose to embark. Rather change is a raging torrent from which there is no escape. The best anyone can do is learn to navigate the currents, keeping afloat and, ideally, staying ahead of the competition. The fact that today Kotter's model is more likely to be illustrated as a never-ending circle rather than a series of steps is just one indication of the changing work environment.

But whatever the context, leading and navigating change has developed into a distinctive and vital part of what people do at work and how they do it. At its heart, this is about keeping up with the times: ensuring that an organisation remains flexible, market- and customer-focused, relevant, appealing and profitable, and inclined to do the right things in the right way at the right time.

In practice

Kotter's eight steps for creating major change still offer a useful roadmap for what leaders need to do to ensure that beneficial change is achieved. The approach highlights many of the skills, ways of thinking and actions that are prerequisites for success.

Establish a sense of urgency

Momentum is everything. To ensure that the need for change is accepted, it is important to remove complacency and inertia and to make a clear case for why change is needed. Often the role of the change leader is to stay positive and build on success, but at this time it also helps to anticipate failure: what might go wrong, how, when, and what the consequences of not taking action could be. It may also help to emphasise specifics, such as windows of opportunity that require swift action. Launching a new product is an example: there really is only one time to create a first impression, so making sure that a launch takes place effectively is essential.

Form a strong guiding coalition

This is a group of strong, unified people who drive the changes and establish support throughout the entire organisation. The guiding coalition needs to understand the purpose of the change: what is required and what it is intended to achieve. As well as being united and bearing cabinet responsibility, this group should be coordinated and have the power to make things happen. In situations requiring fast change – a major reputational risk crisis, for example – a single team skilled at making decisions affecting the whole organisation is vital.

Create a vision

A clear sense of direction and a sense of the end result will focus the efforts of everyone involved. Two points are useful to remember. First, it is psychologically easier to move towards something positive than to move away from a negative. Second, the vision needs to be practical and guiding, and needs to influence the actions that are being taken across the board.

Communicate the vision

The vision for the change – what it means and why it matters – must be explained to everyone involved. The aim is to secure engagement and support as widely as possible. It helps to communicate the new vision and approach constantly and consistently, using the most appropriate media and communication styles. This will then start to build pressure, momentum and understanding, sustaining the sense of urgency. Boards of directors, for example, sometimes struggle to understand why their vision is failing to deliver the intended results, ignoring the fact that they have failed to engage colleagues with what the vision means in practice for people, and how they need to change in response to it.

Empower people to act in line with the vision

Even the strongest guiding coalition cannot change their

organisation on their own. Change needs to come from the grassroots upwards, and this is best accomplished by encouraging people to act in a supportive, inclusive environment, with everyone pulling in the same direction. To empower people, leaders need to make sure that they remove obstacles (including intangible attitudes and beliefs); change systems or structures that undermine the vision; and encourage new thinking and (calculated) risk-taking.

Create short-term wins

Short-term wins matter because they highlight what is required as well as the value of the change; they generate momentum, and they provide an opportunity to build on success. When Amazon first started operating, Jeff Bezos installed a bell in the office that would ring every time an order was received. Within a week the bell was disconnected to stop the constant ringing, and the message was clear: success – and change – were coming.

Consolidate improvements and maintain momentum

This part of the process is arguably the hardest: the initial excitement will have passed, some goals will have been achieved, and people know what is required. But change fatigue may have kicked in and there may be a lack of enthusiasm to address problems as they arise. The key is to move steadily: to maintain momentum without pushing too fast which could destabilise the change process. It can help to use recent successes to reinvigorate the process of change. It's also important to up-skill and develop people or to hire new people to implement the vision.

Institutionalise the new approaches

Kotter recognised that one of the key dangers when leading people through a time of change is finishing too early. You may think that new IT system has been implemented but, before you know it, everyone has gone back to using their own spreadsheets. You need to keep going to make sure the change is properly bedded in. What matters is that the changes are firmly grounded in the organisation, and that everyone understands what has been gained and where the process might continue to go in the future.

Thought starters

- What changes do you want to make in your working life or career? What would be the ideal?
- How will you gather support, generate momentum and achieve your goal?
- What broader changes do you want to make in your organisation? Is there a clear vision of the future state, as well as a strategy for achieving that vision?
- Is the guiding coalition unified, supportive and focused on their objectives as a team?
- How will you sustain the change beyond the short term?

What next?

Read *Leading Change* by John Kotter.

15

The Eisenhower matrix

Managing priorities and workload

The big picture

The Eisenhower matrix, also known as the Eisenhower urgent/ important matrix, is a productivity tool and time management method attributed to the 34th President of the United States, Dwight D. Eisenhower. The matrix is designed to help people prioritise tasks and activities based on their levels of urgency and importance, thereby improving efficiency and focus.

The Eisenhower matrix is a visual aid that helps people to make more informed decisions about how they allocate their time and effort. By using the matrix, you can avoid the trap of constantly reacting to urgent but less important tasks and instead invest your energy in activities that align better with your goals and objectives. For example, rather than constantly reading and responding to emails as they pop into your in-box, you could instead prioritise deep work or time for reflection that may not be so urgent but is often more important.

By using the Eisenhower matrix, you can improve your productivity, reduce stress, and achieve a better work–life balance by focusing on what truly matters.

About the idea

The matrix, shown in Figure 2, organises tasks into four quadrants based on two criteria: urgency and importance. It advises the action you should take for each.

1. Urgent and important: do first.
2. Important but not urgent: schedule.
3. Urgent but not important: delegate.
4. Not urgent and not important: eliminate.

Quadrant 1. Urgent and important: do first

Tasks in this quadrant are both urgent and important and require immediate attention. They often involve critical deadlines, emergencies or pressing issues. Prioritising and addressing tasks in this quadrant quickly is essential.

Examples include preparing for a client presentation that's taking place tomorrow and attending an important strategy meeting with your manager.

Quadrant 2. Important but not urgent: schedule

Tasks in this quadrant are important but do not require immediate attention. They are long-term goals, strategic planning, personal development and activities that contribute to growth and success. Although not urgent, spending time on tasks in this quadrant can make a significant difference to you and your colleagues.

Figure 2: **The Eisenhower urgent/important matrix**

	Urgent	Not urgent
Important	**1. Do first** Important and urgent	**2. Schedule** Important but not urgent
Not important	**3. Delegate** Not important but urgent	**4. Eliminate** Not important and not urgent

Examples include planning and executing a strategic marketing campaign, team appraisals and studying to acquire new skills.

Quadrant 3. Urgent but not important: delegate

Tasks in this quadrant are urgent but not important in the grand scheme of things. They might be distractions, interruptions, or requests from other people that take effort away from more critical tasks. Delegating or outsourcing these tasks can free up time for more meaningful work.

Examples include attending routine meetings and administrative tasks that could be done by others or automated.

Quadrant 4. Not urgent and not important: eliminate

Tasks in this quadrant are neither urgent nor important and often represent time-wasting activities, trivial matters or unnecessary distractions. It's best to eliminate or minimise the time spent on these type of tasks to focus on more valuable endeavours.

Examples include scrolling through social media, and spending time on unproductive activities that offer little or no value. Does anyone ever read that report you always run on a Friday? If not, stop running it.

The matrix can also be used with other time management tools – for example, timeboxing, which involves filling up your diary by allocating a fixed amount of time for each task (as well as things like a proper lunch break or time for reflection) and assigning ABC labels to tasks to indicate priority.

There are many benefits of applying and using the Eisenhower matrix.

- *Enhancing productivity.* By focusing on the most important tasks and reducing time-wasting activities, you can be more productive and achieve better results.

- *Improving decision-making.* The matrix provides a clear framework for making decisions about where to allocate your time and energy, ensuring you invest in what truly matters.

- *Managing and potentially reducing stress.* Addressing urgent and important tasks promptly can reduce the stress caused by looming deadlines and last-minute rushes.
- *Aligning goals.* The matrix helps align your activities with your long-term goals, promoting progress and success in various areas of your life.
- *Optimising your use of time.* By differentiating between urgent and important tasks, you can optimise your time and create a more balanced schedule.

In practice

How can you best use the Eisenhower matrix for improving time management, productivity and decision-making?

Consider first what your own short-, medium- and long-term objectives are. These might be personal and organisational goals to be completed this week, this month and this quarter. Think about the tasks required to achieve those objectives and whether they are urgent or not urgent, and whether they can be delegated. There will also be tasks that you are asked to perform that do not directly help you achieve your goals but are still important, such as collaboration with another team or mentoring someone. Once you have a clear sense of your objectives and obligations, you can start to prioritise with confidence.

List tasks

Start by listing all the tasks and activities you need to accomplish, whether for work, personal life, or any other area.

Categorise tasks

Place each task into one of the four quadrants based on its urgency and importance. Be honest and objective when making these assessments.

Focus on quadrant 1

Begin by tackling tasks in quadrant 1. These tasks require immediate attention, so prioritise them to prevent negative consequences. This might include responding to a vital request from a colleague or customer.

Plan for quadrant 2

Allocate time for quadrant 2 tasks. These activities contribute to your long-term goals and should be given dedicated time and attention. This might include preparing for an upcoming meeting or presentation, managing colleagues or other stakeholders, or time for reflection.

Delegate quadrant 3

Evaluate tasks in quadrant 3 and determine if any can be delegated to others, freeing up your time to focus on more important responsibilities. This might include asking a colleague to attend a meeting on your behalf.

Minimise quadrant 4

Identify tasks in quadrant 4 and try to minimise or eliminate them. Avoid getting caught up in time-wasting activities.

Regularly review and update your task list as priorities may change

Stay adaptable and adjust your focus accordingly. The key to successful implementation is consistency. Using the Eisenhower matrix consistently will help you to focus on what matters at that particular time.

Thought starters

- How easily can you list your objectives and obligations for the next three months?

- Reflect on how the Eisenhower matrix might help you identify and prioritise tasks that align with your long-term goals and values.
- How can quadrant 2 tasks, which are important but not urgent, be scheduled and given appropriate attention to avoid them becoming urgent later?
- How can the matrix be applied around quadrant 3 to delegate tasks effectively and enhance overall team productivity?
- What strategies can you implement to minimise or eliminate time-wasting activities in quadrant 4 of the matrix?

What next?

Read *Eat That Frog! Get More of the Important Things Done Today* by Brian Tracy.

16

Covey's seven habits of highly effective people

Achieving personal improvement and greater success

The big picture

In 1989 one of the most famous personal development books of all time was published: Stephen R. Covey's *The 7 Habits of Highly Effective People: Powerful Lessons in Personal Change.* The book's influence was considerable: it encouraged people to improve their effectiveness at work, and Covey showed that the market for insights encouraging greater personal effectiveness and fulfilment was here to stay. Since his work was first produced, publishers have provided a steady stream of career and life-enhancing insights from a wide range of thinkers.

Covey himself was heavily influenced by the works of management thinker Peter Drucker, as well as Carl Rogers, one of the driving forces behind psychotherapy in the US. Another major influence on Covey's thinking was his own study of American self-help books that he completed for his doctoral dissertation. Covey was closely affiliated with the Church of Jesus Christ of Latter-day Saints, and commentators have remarked that the seven habits can be seen as a secular distillation of the Latter-day Saint values.

About the idea

The 7 Habits of Highly Effective People outlines a set of activities and attitudes that result in greater personal effectiveness, fulfilment and success.

1. *Be proactive.* This involves self-determination, the power to decide the best response to a situation, controlling your environment.

2. *Begin with the end in mind.* To achieve your aims, concentrate on those activities that are most relevant to achieving your end goals. This will help you keep focused, avoid distractions and be more productive and successful.

3. *Put first things first.* Effective personal management involves organising and implementing activities that will help you to achieve your aims. Prioritise and then take action.

4. *Think win–win.* Personal success invariably requires interpersonal skills and productive relationships, as progress and success often depend on the cooperation and support of others. Covey argues that win-win is based on two assumptions: there is plenty for everyone, and success tends to follow a cooperative rather than a confrontational approach.

5. *Seek first to understand, then to be understood.* Covey argues that personal success requires understanding, sound judgement and clear communication. It's important to "diagnose before you prescribe".

6. *Synergise.* Achieving improvements in personal effectiveness, Covey argues, requires creative cooperation. Understanding two issues is important here: first, the principle that the whole is greater than the sum of the parts: you can achieve more by working together. Second, when you work together, you need to organise in such a way that uses each person's strengths. This means seeing both the good and the potential in the other person's contribution.

7. *Sharpen the saw.* Self-awareness, reflection and a desire to sustain our equilibrium are all crucial to enabling and strengthening habits. This approach, described by Covey as "self-renewal", is achieved by dividing oneself into four constituent parts – spiritual, mental, physical and

social/emotional – all of which are essential for sustained effectiveness.

In his 2004 book *The 8th Habit: From Effectiveness to Greatness*, Covey added one further habit leading to greater personal effectiveness, fulfilment and success: find your voice and inspire others to find theirs.

In practice

The seven habits are still relevant today, drawing on long-standing expectations and views of what makes people effective and successful at work. It also helps that they are habits: targeted actions that can be adapted to your own situation and that, with commitment and practice, accumulate over time to deliver a powerful level of expertise and self-belief. This makes the habits feel *achievable*.

To apply the seven habits, consider which areas would provide you with the greatest benefit.

Here are some questions you could ask yourself.

1. *Be proactive.* Where could you be more proactive? Are there "lurkers" (unpleasant issues that you have been avoiding) that need to be resolved?

2. *Begin with the end in mind.* What is your priority at the moment? What will success look like, and how will it feel?

3. *Put first things first.* What will you stop doing to make way for new activities? What changes do you need to make in what you know, do and believe?

4. *Think win–win.* Are you clear about who else will benefit from your achievements? How invested are they in your success?

5. *Seek first to understand, then to be understood.* Are your motives and goals clearly understood? How do you come across? How well do you understand your colleagues' priorities, goals and concerns?

6. *Synergise.* How well do you understand and use the strengths of the people around you? What more could you do to encourage and support them?

7. *Sharpen the saw.* Are you open to new ideas and ways of working? How well do you look after yourself? What more could you do to support and sustain yourself?

Thought starters

- What is the one new thing you could do that, if done regularly, would make a positive difference in your *personal* life?
- What one new thing could you do regularly that would have the greatest beneficial impact in your *work* life?
- Which of the seven habits could you do more often or better than at present?
- Which of the seven habits would benefit from sharing with others, encouraging a collective habit?
- What more could you do to follow the eighth habit – to find your voice and inspire others to find theirs?

What next?

Read *The 7 Habits of Highly Effective People* by Stephen Covey.

17

Sun Tzu's *The Art of War*

Timeless insights for competing effectively

The big picture

The Art of War is an ancient military treatise attributed to Sun Tzu, a Chinese military general, strategist and philosopher. Dating from the 5th century BC, the text has 13 chapters, each of which is devoted to a different aspect of strategic warfare. It is considered one of the most important works on strategy and has influenced leaders around the world in terms of military thinking, business tactics, legal strategy, politics, sports, lifestyles and beyond.

Although the book was written more than 2,500 years ago, Sun Tzu's work is widely admired for its practical approach to strategy, as well as its emphasis on understanding the enemy and the larger context in which a conflict takes place. It also emphasises the importance of adapting to changing circumstances and using both deception and surprise to gain advantage.

The Art of War offers a set of principles and strategies that can be applied to a range of work situations. For example, the idea of gathering and analysing information about the competition, understanding the broader context in which a business operates, and adapting to changing circumstances are all concepts that resonate in the world of work today.

About the idea

The Art of War contains several key concepts.

The importance of having a clear and realistic goal. Sun Tzu emphasises that this is vital to guide the actions of troops (team members) and ensure that resources are used effectively.

The value of gathering and analysing information, including as much detail as possible about the enemy (competitors), the terrain (competitive environment), and the larger context in which a conflict takes place (business environment). He also emphasises the importance of analysing this information to make informed decisions.

The importance of discipline and unity, ensuring that people work effectively together and follow the orders they are given.

The need to choose the right moment to attack or defend. Sun Tzu advises military leaders to choose the right moment based on their own strengths and weaknesses, as well as those of the enemy. He also emphasises the importance of adapting to changing circumstances to maintain an advantage. This emphasis on avoiding unnecessary conflict and maintaining good relations with allies is as relevant to business relationships and negotiations today as it was 26 centuries ago.

The Art of War is, of course, a product of its time and place and its principles and strategies are certainly not applicable to all cultures and contexts today. Its deterministic focus on conflict and victory may also seem out of step with a world of work built increasingly on collaboration and cooperation. Factors such as strength, strategy, and the ability to gather and analyse information may not adequately account for the role of chance, oppositional defiance and unpredictability, whether at war or at work.

That said, *The Art of War* remains a classic work, encapsulating principles that continue to be useful to modern businesses looking to succeed in competitive environments.

In practice

The Art of War's philosophical approach is applicable to various aspects of life, including business, politics and sports. These are several ways to apply *The Art of War* to aspects of your personal and professional life.

Understand your own (and your competitors') strengths and weaknesses

Make sure you have a thorough understanding of the situation before making a move. A classic example is applying for a new job role: the challenge is not only to show how your skills and experience will fit the role and benefit the employer, but also to be distinctive and memorable, looking to stand out in your application.

Use strategy and planning to your advantage

Sun Tzu argued that a well-planned strategy is more effective than relying on brute force alone. The equivalent is sending a sales team into the market with ambitious targets without considering other ways to reach customers. Teamworking in general – and working as part of a project team in particular – is an instance where an agreed plan and approach (including roles, timescales, actions, behaviours) is invaluable.

Be flexible and adaptable

These are qualities that are still hugely significant in the 21st century. Sun Tzu emphasised the importance of being able to adapt to changing circumstances. In the face of global climate change, for example, organisations are adapting their operations to reduce carbon emissions, which is now a factor in decision-making.

Seek to win without fighting

The best victory is one that can be achieved without resorting to violence or conflict. For example, negotiating a pre-emptive "win–win" solution (see Chapter 50) where all sides benefit, is generally preferable to trying to "win" at someone else's expense.

Use deception and surprise to your advantage

By disguising your intentions and using unexpected tactics, you can gain a crucial advantage over your opponent. These kinds of stealth tactics have been used by businesses such as low-cost airlines, targeting under-served customers in "low-end market footholds" (see Chapter 27 on disruptive innovation). Other airlines initially dismissed these new entrants, until they started reshaping the market.

Keep your objectives in mind at all times

Have a clear understanding of your goals and stay focused on achieving them.

Know when to retreat

It is better to retreat and regroup rather than to continue fighting and risk losing everything. Beware, for example, the "sunk-cost trap" where people continue investing resources regardless of changing circumstances, on the grounds that so much has already been spent. The solution is to recognise the loss, stop making a bad situation worse, and retreat.

Always be aware of the bigger picture

Consider long-term consequences, rather than just focusing on the immediate situation. A modern example of this principle in action is the rise of business networks such as LinkedIn. People generally recognise that staying connected with people delivers much more than short-term transactional benefits – the bigger picture is that connections can help throughout a career and in ways that you may not even be clear about when the connection is first made.

Thought starters

- Take time to understand and update your view of your strengths and weaknesses. What more could you do to play to your strengths, and minimise the effects of your weaknesses?
- How well do you really know your competitors? What sources of information do you have and how often do you analyse them?

- What would "seek to win without fighting" look like for you or your organisation?
- How would visualising the competitive landscape as a battlefield change your perspective and attitude to strategy?
- How skilled are you at taking a big picture view – for example, understanding broader issues, contexts, trends and their implications – as well as focusing on the immediate situation?

What next?

Read *The Art of War by* Sun Tzu.

18

Blue ocean strategy

Creating an original, disruptive and uncontested business

The big picture

Developed by Chan Kim and Renée Mauborgne, two professors of strategy at INSEAD, the central idea of blue ocean strategy is that instead of competing directly with competitors in an existing market, organisations should focus on finding new markets.

There are several reasons for this approach, but the most compelling is clear: the opportunity to create a monopoly and reap the returns before competitors enter the new market you have created. Examples include the rise of disruptive businesses and innovators such as Apple, Airbnb and Amazon.

Kim and Mauborgne identified their approach to strategy based on a study of 150 strategic business moves spanning more than 100 years across 30 sectors. Their insights were first published in 2004 in a *Harvard Business Review* article, and then in 2005 in their book *Blue Ocean Strategy*.

About the idea

Blue Ocean Strategy outlines two attitudes to competition: red oceans and blue oceans. The current marketplace for all products and services are made up of *red oceans* (bloody battlegrounds) where boundaries are clearly defined, and organisations operate within them. Here, organisations compete to gain extra share within the current market.

In contrast, *blue oceans* are areas of deep, uncharted, almost limitless potential where the aim is not to compete conventionally but to develop products and services that create entirely new markets: in essence, creating customers that do not yet exist.

Examples of blue ocean strategy in action include:

- *low-cost airlines* which recognised that many people want to travel in a way that is inexpensive and fun, not costly and stuffy
- *Cirque du Soleil* which reinvented the waning concept of a circus by presenting it as a stage show
- *streaming services* – notably Spotify and Netflix – which developed initially uncontested markets for on-demand music, podcasts and videos.

In practice

Blue ocean strategy is about moving an organisation to a place where it can rapidly grow and increase profits with little or no competition. This typically requires a shift in thinking, together with the application of several principles.

Shift your thinking

Kim and Mauborgne emphasise the need for a bold mindset willing to defy conventional wisdom about value and cost. Most organisations operate in the red ocean, focusing on the need for trade-offs between creating more value for the customer at greater cost, or creating less value at a lower cost. Food retailers and hotel companies are a classic example of this: either providing "value" ranges at a low cost, or "premium" offerings at a greater cost.

Blue ocean organisations do not accept that there needs to be such a trade-off. Instead, they create value, often at a lower cost, through products and services that appeal to a new market of customers.

The authors highlight three shifts needed to move successfully towards a blue ocean mindset.

1. *Develop a blue ocean perspective.* This is possibly the toughest challenge: overcoming existing convention and thinking. In an established organisation this can be particularly difficult because you need to think like a start-up and focus not on competing in a market, but on *creating* a market.

2. *Use market-creating tools and insights.* You need to apply the right practical tools. In particular, this means asking the right questions at the right time and understanding the significance of the answers. This is best done in collaboration within a diverse and supportive group, who can provide different perspectives, challenge orthodoxy and build on each other's thinking.

3. *Recognise that the mindset is fundamentally about people.* Sailing into a blue ocean is invariably a risky venture, literally taking an uncharted course. This requires personal attributes including courage, confidence, mutual support, a willingness to accept challenge and adapt.

4. Several other qualities also matter, notably *empathy*, understanding how colleagues, customers and others are feeling; *communication*, to ensure that momentum is sustained and people are moving together in the same direction; and *learning*, so people have the required levels of confidence and competence to succeed.

Understand that technology is an enabler, not a panacea

Kim and Mauborgne highlight the fact that technological innovation is rarely the key defining characteristic of blue oceans. Instead, blue ocean companies typically use existing technologies to redesign a product, service or method of delivery, creating a new offering as a result.

Challenge existing market boundaries

Reimagine the market by identifying new customers. These may be customers that are not yet served or are inadequately served.

Keep focused on the overall picture

What matters and needs to be achieved.

Minimise risk

Assess current industry practices and decide what can be eliminated, improved, reduced (either simplified or not done to existing standards), or offered for the first time.

Implement the plan carefully and creatively

Succeeding with a blue ocean strategy requires an ability to overcome barriers, secure resources and support, and remain resilient and committed despite your unorthodox approach being challenged.

An interesting example of the thoughtful, bold approach needed to make a blue ocean strategy work is provided by the Australian wine company Casella Wines and its brand Yellow Tail. Established in 2001, the small, unknown brand decided not to compete in the traditional wine drinking markets against French and Italian producers. Instead, Yellow Tail set out to create new wine consumers in the US. It adopted a different marketing approach to the established wine producers, offering a wine that was unpretentious, accessible, fun and easy to drink. In fact, it wasn't competing with other wines for social drinkers, but with beer and cocktail drinkers. In 2001 Casella expected to sell 25,000 cases a year; by the end of 2005 the company's cumulative sales were over 25 million cases.

Thought starters

- What does everyone in your industry do in the same way? What are the standard ways of working, assumptions and best practices that everyone follows?
- Where are the gaps? Which industry standards could your organisation redefine when creating a new service or product?

- What might disappoint or frustrate current and potential customers about existing products or services that you could address?
- What industry standards could be eliminated or adapted to save costs and/or time?
- What problems are you likely to face when implementing your blue ocean strategy? How might you address them?

What next?

Read *Blue Ocean Strategy: How to Create Uncontested Market Space and Make the Competition Irrelevant* by W. Chan Kim and Renée A. Mauborgne.

19

Porter's five forces: competitive strategy

Understanding how market forces determine competitive advantage

The big picture

Porter's five forces framework is widely used to analyse the operating environment and competitive forces facing a business and industry. First published in 1979 by Michael Porter in the *Harvard Business Review*, the five forces framework analyses the forces that shape an industry and determine the intensity of competition and, as a result, potential profitability.

The framework helps businesses to understand the competitive landscape, with particular focus on the forces that affect profitability, and to then develop strategies to succeed in the market. The idea is that by understanding and addressing these factors, organisations can increase their insights and competitive advantage, thus improving their chances of success. The framework can be used across all industries and sectors to support strategic development and deployment.

About the idea

The five forces are listed below.

1. Threat of new entrants

This refers to the likelihood that new companies will enter the market and compete with existing firms, if the barriers to entry are low enough. If it takes relatively little time, money or other resources, or if key technologies or other intellectual property are unprotected or easily replicated, then rivals can easily enter your market and weaken your position.

2. Bargaining power of buyers

This refers to the ability of customers to negotiate prices or demand higher quality products and services. Buyers' bargaining power is usually strong if you have relatively few buyers in the market and they have a choice about who to buy from, or if you have a large number of buyers but only a few account for a high proportion of your sales (for example, 20% of buyers may account for 80% of revenue). Conversely, if you have many customers and relatively little competition then buyer bargaining power decreases.

3. Bargaining power of suppliers

This refers to the ability of your suppliers to negotiate prices or demand better terms from the organisations they supply to or reduce the quality of their product. If there are fewer suppliers and you rely heavily on them, the stronger their position is and the greater their ability to affect your business and profitability. The world has recently witnessed the bargaining power of those businesses that supply energy and increased costs and improved their profits but damaged profit margins for businesses that could not pass on the increase to their own customers.

4. Threat of substitutes

This refers to the availability of alternative products or services that could potentially replace the ones offered by a company. Simply put, customers could find a product or service that may be cheaper, or better, or both. This happens most often when customers find it easy to switch to another product or when a new and desirable product enters the market. As a result of rising energy costs, for example, consumers have been attracted to air fryers which, in many homes, have become a substitute for a conventional oven because they are cheaper to run.

5. Rivalry among existing competitors

This refers to the intensity of competition among existing organisations in the market. In a market where rivalry is intense, competitors can attract your customers by cutting prices aggressively, providing special offers and launching high-impact marketing campaigns. On the other hand, if competitive rivalry is limited, your competitive power and profitability will be stronger. For example, there is rarely intense rivalry in the high-end clothing market.

Porter's five forces framework has proved to be a useful diagnostic for organisations to assess their competitive standing in their markets and to develop strategies to improve their competitive position. For example, you might find ways to reduce the threat of new entrants, increase the bargaining power of buyers or suppliers, or develop new products or services that are less vulnerable to substitutes. You might also look for ways to differentiate yourself from competitors and create a unique value proposition that sets you apart.

In practice

Here are some things to consider when using the five forces framework.

Putting the framework into practice

Identify the key players in your industry

This should include competitors, buyers, suppliers and potential new entrants.

Dig deeper

Evaluate in detail the range and type of factors affecting competitiveness including, for example: barriers to entry, negotiating power of buyers and suppliers, availability of substitutes, intellectual property protections, and the intensity of competition among existing firms. Determine how each force affects the company's competitive position, as well as the size and scale of each force in turn. This impact may be positive (strengthening the competitive position), negative or negligible.

Use this information

With this picture in mind, the challenge is to decide how to use this information to improve the company's competitive position.

A classic example of a new market entrant systematically dismantling the competitiveness of a market leader is the Japanese technology firm Canon and the photocopier market. Historically the market was dominated by the US corporation Xerox, which invented the industry in the 1960s. Xerox's colossal machines were expensive and needed regular servicing (an additional revenue stream for the company); the machines produced large numbers of copies, and they were sold via distributors with long contracts.

Canon was the upstart: it disrupted the market by designing copiers for maximum reliability, making replacement parts modular so that customers could replace them, and creating designs that were so simple that dealers could be trained to make repairs. Canon's copiers were also priced for organisations of all sizes and were viable even for single copies. The approach meant that Xerox failed to sustain its competitive advantage.

Take the wider view

There are several potential risks associated with using Porter's five forces framework. Like the framework itself, these should be taken in context and applied appropriately. The following considerations will help.

Consider all the external factors

Porter's five forces focuses on internal industry dynamics at a point in time, usually the present. However, there are many external factors that may be felt by the five forces in the near future – such as economic conditions, regulatory changes and technological advancements – and these should also be considered when developing a competitive strategy.

Consider the influence of other stakeholders

In addition to competitors, buyers, suppliers and potential new entrants, there are other stakeholders, such as employees, investors and the local community, which can also influence a company's competitive position. It is important to consider the perspectives and interests of these stakeholders when developing a competitive strategy.

Make sure the analysis is up to date

As the market and industry evolve, the strength and relative importance of each of the five forces changes. It is important to regularly reassess the analysis and adjust strategies as needed to stay competitive.

Management writer Rita Gunther McGrath has argued that Porter's five forces framework is outdated and incomplete. In her book *The End of Competitive Advantage* McGrath argues that leaders should pursue what she terms *transient competitive advantage*. In her view, businesses need to seize opportunities fast and exploit them quickly, and then move on to new opportunities before they start to become a liability.

The truth lies in the detail: what matters is the specific context of each business, the nature of its competitors, the strength and enduring appeal (or not) of its offer, its brand, leadership, future plans, resources, and much else besides. Understanding these forces – what and where they are as well as their significance – is revealed by Porter's approach. In many fast-moving sectors, McGrath's approach is likely to be relevant too. But for many organisations, Porter's five forces framework remains a powerful and respected tool that can be used as part of a broader strategic planning process.

Thought starters

- How sensitive is your market to pricing?
- To what extent is your organisation in competitive rivalry?
- Is your profitability affected by buyer or supplier bargaining power? If so, are there actions you can take to mitigate this?
- What alternatives do your customers have for the products or services you offer?
- How could you increase the value of your product or service to the customer, which would lead to competitive advantage and/or price inflation?

What next?

Read *Competitive Strategy: Techniques for Analyzing Industries and Competitors* by Michael Porter.

20

The business model canvas

A simple methodology for strategic planning

The big picture

Alexander Osterwalder's business model canvas is a strategic management tool that provides a visual framework for describing, analysing and designing a business model. It was introduced by Osterwalder and Yves Pigneur in their book *Business Model Generation.*

After introducing the idea in their book, the authors made the concept freely available for public use, encouraging entrepreneurs, start-ups and businesses to use the business model canvas to develop and iterate their business ideas and to understand their business model in a clear and concise way.

Since its publication, a wide range of entrepreneurs and business leaders have used the business model canvas to brainstorm, map out and iterate their business ideas. Among the many advantages of the tool is its applicability across the board: from large enterprises to small start-ups. The visual nature of the canvas allows for easy collaboration, understanding and communication of complex business models. It is a practical tool, helping businesses align their activities by illustrating potential trade-offs and synergies between different parts of their business.

About the idea

Traditional business plans can be lengthy and complex documents, making it difficult to grasp the fundamental aspects of a strategy quickly. The business model canvas provides a practical and visual framework to understand, design and innovate business models and business plans, especially for new products and initiatives.

It simplifies this process by breaking down the organisation into nine key building blocks, as shown in Figure 3. This helps to focus on the essential elements that will drive success.

Perhaps counterintuitively, Osterwalder recommends that people use the canvas from right to left, starting with customer segments.

1. *Customer segments*: the different types of customers an organisation aims to serve.

2. *Customer relationships*: the type of relationship the organisation will establish with its customer segments, for example, personal assistance to self-service.

3. *Channels*: how the organisation communicates with and reaches its customer segments to deliver its value proposition.

Figure 3: **The Business Model Canvas**

Designed for:		Designed by:		Date:	Version:	
Key partners	🔗	Value propositions	🎁	Customer relationships		❤️
Key resources	🏛️	Channels	🚚	Customer segments		🙂
Key activites	✅	Cost structure	🏷️	Revenue Streams		💰

4. *Value propositions*: the unique value or benefits the organisation can offer its customers.

5. *Revenue streams*: how you will generate revenue from each customer segment, such as sales, rentals, subscription fees and licensing.

6. *Key activities*: the most important things you must do to make the business model work and enable the delivery of the value proposition, reaching customers and maintaining relationships.

7. *Key resources*: the most important assets required to make the model work, including physical, intellectual, human and financial resources.

8. *Key partners*: the network of suppliers and partners required to make the business model work. These can optimise operations, reduce risk or acquire resources.

9. *Cost structure*: the costs that will be incurred to operate the business model, including fixed costs (eg, premises, employees) and variable costs (eg, marketing, travel).

In practice

The business model canvas is ideal for a creative thinking workshop that includes representation from across the company to explore ideas and share opinions. It works especially well in start-up businesses, or larger organisations looking to develop new products.

Before starting, it helps to focus on an idea, likely framed as a question. How can you serve your customers better? What would make your customers more loyal? How can you penetrate a new market? How can you use your skills to develop a new product?

Generate ideas

Start by thinking of ideas in a creative and collaborative way. Identify potential customer segments, value propositions and revenue streams.

Complete the canvas

Use the business model canvas template to document your ideas. Fill out each of the nine building blocks with as much detail as possible.

Visualise

Visualise your business model on a physical board or by using software tools. This visual representation helps to understand the relationships between the different components on the canvas.

Validate and test

Create a minimum viable product (MVP) based on your canvas. This could be a prototype, a simple version of your product, or a service offering.

Use the MVP to test your assumptions about customer segments, value propositions and channels. Gather feedback from real users to validate or invalidate your hypotheses.

Iterate

Based on the feedback, iterate on your canvas. Be prepared to make significant changes to your canvas and business model if the feedback suggests it is necessary.

Implement and scale

- *Resource allocation.* Allocate your key resources and activities according to your canvas. This might involve hiring specific talent, investing in technology, or building partnerships.
- *Marketing and sales.* Develop marketing strategies and sales techniques aligned with your channels, customer relationships and value propositions.
- *Revenue generation.* Implement your revenue streams. This could involve setting up online sales, subscription services, or other forms of revenue generation.

- *Scale.* As your business grows, continually revisit your canvas. Scaling might require adjustments in key resources, activities or partnerships.

Monitor and adapt
- *Performance metrics.* Define key performance indicators related to your canvas elements (see Chapter 39). Monitor them to assess the performance of your business model.
- *Feedback loop.* Maintain a feedback loop with customers, employees and stakeholders. Regular feedback can highlight areas for improvement.
- *Continuous adaptation.* Markets change, technologies evolve and customer preferences shift. Revisit your canvas regularly, especially when facing significant changes in your business environment.

Communicate
- *Internal communication.* Use the canvas to align your team. It provides a common language and understanding of your business model.
- *External communication.* When seeking investments or partnerships, use the canvas to explain your business model clearly and concisely to potential investors or collaborators.

It is worth remembering that completing the business model canvas should not be viewed as a one-time activity; it should be considered a living document that is regularly updated and adapted as your business evolves, learning from the market. Regularly revisiting and revising your canvas ensures that your business model remains relevant and effective in the face of changing circumstances and market demands.

Thought starters
- What idea or innovation would benefit from the business model canvas?

- Do your product strategies or business plans have a clear, segmented view of each of the elements that will drive success?

- What are the implications of your business model canvas? For example, do you need a stronger brand, people with a specific skill, more or better distributors? What are the qualitative implications?

- What type of relationship do you want to establish with your customers and which channel will you use to reach them?

- What are the different ways you can generate revenue and what major costs do you need to consider?

What next?

Read *Business Model Generation* by Alexander Osterwalder and Yves Pigneur.

21
SWOT and PEST analysis

Understanding context and seeing the big picture

The big picture

SWOT analysis is a framework that helps organisations identify business or product internal Strengths and Weaknesses, and external Opportunities and Threats. It first emerged with the growth of the idea of strategic planning. In 1965 Robert Stewart, Otis Benepe and Arnold Mitchell at the Stanford Research Institute's Long Range Planning Service described how managers could assess operational issues by grouping them into four components: "satisfactory" present state operations, potential or known "opportunities" in future operations, "faults" in existing operations, and potential or known "threats" to future operations. By the end of the 1960s the four components of SWOT had appeared in a wide range of publications on strategic planning, it came to be referenced widely in lectures, and from then became part of the workplace lexicon.

SWOT is used as a strategic analysis tool to assess internal capabilities and how these affect strategic direction.

PEST analysis, developed in 1967 by Francis Aguilar, an academic at Harvard Business School, is focused on the *external* factors that might influence that strategy. PEST is an environmental scanning framework that can help companies interrogate the wider context within which they operate. Aguilar argued that companies must pay close attention to political, economic, sociocultural and technological (PEST) issues because they can affect strategy profoundly and decisively.

The two frameworks are complementary and continue to form

the basis of both large- and small-scale strategic thinking, whether you're debating the future of an existing product or service or contemplating a major expansion into a new territory.

About the ideas

SWOT and PEST analyses are useful ways to evaluate the most significant forces shaping the future for a product or an organisation. SWOT can also be used to help individuals identify and plot personal goals. As well as being useful tools they have a broader value as part of a process of assessment, reflection and planning. They ensure that these processes take account of internal and external issues as well as current and evolving trends and forces. It is this ability to assess the future and to balance external, internal and current issues that has made these two tools so durable during times of economic opportunity, challenge and change.

Interestingly, part of their strength, versatility and appeal is also a potential weakness: they are simple and swift to prepare – a single workshop session is often all that is needed. Although this is useful for initiating discussion and ideas it can be limiting in terms of rigour, and the outcomes of each analysis are only as good as the knowledge of the individuals who contribute. SWOT and PEST analyses are also stand-alone techniques, so once the ideas have been generated there is no process or requirement to follow through and reflect them in the broader process of strategic planning. However, provided they are not used in isolation, they can provide a useful jumping-off point for planning and action.

In practice

Developing a SWOT analysis

There are several steps to completing and using an effective SWOT analysis but the first is to agree on the subject of the SWOT. This could be an entire organisation, a team or function, a product or service. It can be useful to drill down from the macro to the micro as the analysis progresses.

Prepare a blank 2 x 2 grid

Start with a blank grid, as shown in Figure 4. Assign one quadrant each for strengths, weaknesses, opportunities and threats. Strengths and weaknesses tend to look at factors that are internal; opportunities and threats look to the outside world. Prepare to consider and list relevant factors for each category. Bear in mind that some issues may appear in more than one box. For example, something that appears to be a threat (such as new technology) could also represent a potential opportunity, which could also highlight a weakness in capability.

Know your strengths

Consider what you believe are the strengths of the organisation or product. For an organisation, these could be its employees, products, customer loyalty, processes or location. Evaluate what the organisation does well relative to its competitors.

Recognise weaknesses

Take an objective view of every aspect of the business. Ask whether, and how, products and services could be improved. Try to identify any area of expertise that is lacking. Be as honest as you can when listing weaknesses. It sometimes helps to get an outside view of

Figure 4: **Template for a SWOT grid**

	Helpful to achieving the objective	Harmful to achieving the objective
Internal origin	**Strengths**	**Weaknesses**
External origin	**Opportunities**	**Threats**

weaknesses: your own perceptions may not always match reality. Be prepared to hear things you may not like, and avoid being defensive.

Identify opportunities

Next, identify external opportunities. These typically include new markets, new technologies, new products and services or enhancements to existing products and services, ceasing products or services, strategic partnerships, joint ventures, divestments, new investment, competitor performance, new suppliers and commercial agreements or political, economic, regulatory and trade developments.

Look out for threats

Think about the worst things that could realistically happen, such as losing your biggest customers or facing a new product better than your own.

Threats vary widely and include industrial action, politics and regulatory issues; economic issues, talent and employment issues; trade restrictions or disruption, innovations from competitors and new entrants (including disruptors); cost and price fluctuations; social and environmental factors; natural disasters, crises and security issues; supply chain challenges, distribution and delivery problems; bad debts; demographic shifts and social changes affecting customer tastes or habits.

How to use your SWOT analysis

After completing the SWOT analysis, reflect on the information you have generated, discussing and prioritising issues. You then have a framework which can feed into strategic planning. Opportunities may become strategic objectives; to deliver those objectives and realise the opportunity, you need to address the weaknesses and threats you have highlighted.

Be aware, too, of the pitfalls of SWOT analysis. These include focusing on just a few, limited issues; completing a SWOT analysis on your own or without a sufficiently diverse set of views; minimising or downplaying weaknesses and threats and using the same analysis for too long. SWOT analyses need to be revisited and updated regularly to make sure they remain relevant and useful.

Looking outwards for opportunities: using a PEST analysis

PEST is a simple framework that enables you to check that strategy and plans have accounted for any external factors. It works well alongside SWOT analysis.

As with SWOT, the best approach is to discuss the issues and group them in columns headed by each of the four PEST categories. Then reflect on each issue in turn, looking to build on opportunities, minimise the impact of threats or changes in the way the business works (for example, changes in regulation or taxation), and prioritise and maximise key opportunities.

PEST factors include the following.

Political

Consider local, national and international policy that could affect your company – from local councils and national governments to supranational bodies and regimes. What, for example, might changes to key legislation or regulation mean for you? Recently, organisations in all sectors have had to address carbon reduction legislation. Changes to labour laws and minimum wage also affect all organisations.

Economic

The next area on which to focus is current and potential financial issues, such as consumer spending, taxation, financial regulation, interest rates and currency markets, as well as issues (such as immigration) that affect labour markets.

Social

Understanding developing social trends is often important for long-term success. Key issues can include changing demographics, confidence in the economy (specifically, consumer confidence), people's values, changes in fashion and expectations about who they do business with.

Technological

The application of new technology is driving many of the changes seen in organisations – fuelling both opportunities (eg, the potential to reduce costs or improve service and delivery), and threats (eg, disruptive new competitors). It is an inescapable fact: organisations that fail to move with new technology risk rapidly becoming outdated, out-competed and obsolete.

You might also want to consider several successful variations of PEST analysis, including PESTLE, which explicitly adds legal and environmental factors. Include these additional factors in your analysis as relevant.

Thought starters

- Would your organisation or team benefit from a new SWOT and/or PEST analysis?
- How could you integrate these analyses into your thinking, planning and measuring?
- Reflect on whether you tend to rely on assumptions or an outdated strategic analysis. If you do, what is the solution?
- How aware are you and your colleagues of relevant shifts in the external environment? How could this improve?
- A personal SWOT assessment is a useful technique for self-development. With this in mind, what are your own greatest strengths, weaknesses, opportunities and threats (or career challenges)?

What next?

View the Mind Tools video "How to use SWOT analysis", or simply try completing one for a key product or your team.

22

The shamrock organisation

Building organisational structures that maximise flexibility

The big picture

Charles Handy is a management thinker, business school professor and author who has written extensively on business and management. One of his most famous concepts is the *shamrock organisation* which he introduced in his book *The Age of Unreason*.

It's an idea that challenges bureaucratic organisational structures characterised by hierarchies of clearly defined roles and responsibilities and centralised decision-making. These structures may be efficient and effective but, Handy argues, they can also be inflexible and slow to respond to change.

Instead, the shamrock organisation is a type of hybrid organisational structure that combines elements of both traditional bureaucratic structures alongside more flexible, less structured ways of working.

Handy's concept of the shamrock organisation provides a model for organisations that is efficient, flexible and capable of adapting to changing conditions. The three-leaf shamrock design guides companies towards a way of working that enables them to adapt quickly to changing demands, reduce fixed costs, and focus on their core competencies while using external resources as needed.

The concept has been influential in the field of management and has helped to shape the way that many companies think about their structure and strategy.

About the idea

The idea is that shamrock organisations are made up of three components.

The first is a *stable core*, represented by the first leaf of the shamrock, which is responsible for essential functions (such as finance, HR and legal), as well as senior managers and professionals. These functions provide stability and direction for the organisation and are typically hierarchical and centralised.

The other two leaves of the shamrock represent the more flexible, dynamic elements of the organisation, which can respond quickly to changing circumstances and take advantage of new opportunities.

The second leaf comprises *contract workers* – individuals who are self-employed contractors or consultants employed on a project basis. They may be more loosely organised and less hierarchical than the core workers, and may be made up of smaller teams, organised around objectives and projects rather than function.

The third leaf Handy defines as comprising *peripheral workers*, the bulk of the workforce who perform routine but often essential work. The demand for their work fluctuates with the fortunes of the business, and there are often only limited career or progression opportunities.

Examples are retailers such as Wal-Mart, Carrefour, Tesco and Amazon. Senior executives set strategy and lead the business, while teams reporting to the heads of the finance, purchasing, people, IT or legal departments are also part of the stable core. Contract workers or consultants may be retained for activities such as brand management, marketing, product launches, IT development, facilities management and others, but these are typically project focused and temporary. The people who are restocking the shelves, processing sales or delivering purchases are peripheral, although clearly they are essential.

The result is a flexible and efficient structure that comprises a core group of essential full-time employees, a periphery of temporary and contract workers, and a network of outsourced services. For example, organisations commonly outsource administrative functions such as facilities management or payroll services. A project team might bring in specialist support on a freelance or fixed-term basis to boost internal expertise as needed. A construction company might recruit more contractors to take on more projects and a retail business might employ additional staff in the run-up to busy holiday periods.

By challenging the notion of conventional hierarchies, Handy opened the door to more flexible ways of thinking about organisational structure, particularly the notion of scaling up and scaling down depending on demand. Through necessity, traditional bureaucracies have eroded and become looser. This has brought both benefits to skilled workers, who enjoy flexibility in how and when their skills are deployed, and challenges for many who have little choice but to navigate the often-difficult world of the gig economy.

However, this shift away from bureaucracy and hierarchy shows little sign of abating. For example, many teams have moved their focus away from being organised around functions or products towards greater autonomy and a focus on customers, markets and channels.

The revolution anticipated by Handy's shamrock organisation has also led to other variations.

Matrix structures are where employees report to both functional and product managers rather than to a single boss. This can allow for greater flexibility and the ability to respond quickly to change.

Network structures, which rely on partnerships and collaboration with other organisations to achieve their goals, have also gained in popularity. This is evident, for example, in the rise of home delivery services where retailers and restaurants have formed partnerships with delivery providers to serve customers.

Flat organisational structures, where there are fewer levels of management and where decision-making is decentralised, are also more common.

The trade-offs between rigid hierarchical structures and less rigid structures can be difficult to manage. Greater flexibility and autonomy can come at the price of greater complexity. Teams can be harder to coordinate, and quality and efficiency risks becoming compromised. Communication can be trickier. Consider the average Zoom meeting with a remote team of people based around the world. People might feel a sense of conflicting loyalties, and engaging and retaining talent may be more difficult.

Ultimately, the best structure for a particular organisation will depend on its specific goals and circumstances. The shamrock is one way to assess the options and allow you to find the structure that best fits your needs.

In practice

Handy's shamrock organisation is a practical way to think about organisational design and where efficiencies can be made. Deciding how to balance organisations between the centre and constituent parts is an enduring challenge.

For example, a US-based consultancy business might face the challenge of what work should be handled directly from the US parent company; what would benefit from outside (non-local) expertise; and what could be assigned to specific, more temporary project teams. Having a more flexible solution that can adapt as circumstances change makes the business more able to adapt to change.

If you think a shamrock-type structure might work for you, consider the following.

Identify the essential functions of the organisation that should be handled by the stable core

This might include activities such as financial management, human resources, IT and legal compliance.

Determine which activities are more flexible and dynamic and can be handled by contractors and consultants

These might include activities such as research and development, marketing and customer service. They are likely to involve a range of employment relationships, including part-time, temporary and flexible.

Put in place systems and processes to make the structure work

Establish clear roles and responsibilities for each part of the organisation's activities, ensuring that there is effective communication and coordination between the three leaves of the shamrock: the stable core, the contract workers and the peripheral workers.

Implementing the shamrock organisation model requires careful planning and a willingness to embrace change and adapt to new circumstances. It can be a complex and challenging process, but it can also provide significant benefits in terms of flexibility in the face of change.

Thought starters

- Consider the benefits and challenges of implementing the shamrock organisation model.
- How could the shamrock organisation model be used to foster innovation and creativity in your company?
- How could the shamrock organisation model be used to improve the efficiency and flexibility of your company?
- What are the potential pitfalls of implementing the shamrock organisation model, and how can they be avoided?
- How could the shamrock organisation model be adapted to fit the specific needs and circumstances of your company?

What next?

Read *The Age of Unreason: New Thinking for a New World* by Charles Handy.

23

Kaizen and business process re-engineering

How to improve in a world of rising expectations

The big picture

Several disparate forces and developments coalesced in the 1980s and early 90s to provide a determined focus on improving quality and service and reducing cost in organisations.

Many of these ideas originated in the rise of Japanese industry and innovation, leading to a desire in the West to learn from Japan's growth and success. At the same time, globalisation, an intensification of competitive market pressures, customers' declining tolerance for poor quality standards, and the enabling effects of technology came together to provide a climate ripe for ideas to drive efficiency and improvement.

One of the most significant outcomes was the spread of total quality management (TQM), an approach defined in 1992 by author Dan Ciampa as consisting of organisation-wide efforts to "install and make permanent a climate where employees continuously improve their ability to provide on-demand products and services that customers will find of particular value".

Two of the most significant components of TQM are *kaizen*, a Japanese approach to ensuring continual improvement through gradual change, and *business process re-engineering*, which focuses on the analysis and design of workflows and business processes to rethink operations that improves customer service, cuts operational costs and sharpens competitiveness.

About the ideas

Kaizen

Kaizen is about making small, gradual and continual improvements to business processes. Originally popularised in the 1980s by Masaaki Imai, a Japanese management consultant, kaizen focuses on achieving organisation-wide quality improvements by involving everyone, at every level. In particular, kaizen recognises that people who use the processes on the ground are best placed to recognise where changes can be made. This belief undermined the need for hierarchical management and, crucially, tapped into a huge source of talent, knowledge and ideas.

By encouraging everyone to improve quality, kaizen promotes teamwork, pride and shared accountability, with people feeling motivated and working towards the same aspirations.

Business process re-engineering

Michael Hammer, an engineer and MIT professor who, with fellow engineer and consultant James Champy, developed the business process re-engineering (BPR) concept, defined re-engineering as "the fundamental rethinking and radical redesign of the business processes to achieve dramatic improvements in critical contemporary measures of performance, such as cost, quality, service and speed".

BPR has three separate elements.

1. *Process improvement*: emphasising small, steady improvements in every aspect of an organisation's activities.

2. *Process re-design*: an approach that uses many of the same techniques as kaizen but is much more concerned with achieving significant step change rather than incremental improvement. To achieve this, it concentrates on processes that cross functional boundaries and constantly asks: "Should we be doing this process at all?"

3. *Process re-engineering*: relies on radical, dramatic change to achieve major breakthroughs in performance – for example,

cutting development and production cycles by 40% to beat competitors.

In recent years TQM and BPR in particular have been criticised for their emphasis on process and rationality, largely at the expense of slack, agility and contingency. For example, widely reported supply chain issues during the covid-19 pandemic have been seen as an example of the pursuit of efficiency at the expense of some much-needed slack. Arguments have also been made that a relentless focus on efficiency means that people have limited time to think, be creative and innovate, which can be detrimental.

More positively, though, achieving significant quality improvements, initially in manufacturing and later in every aspect of organisational life, has led to an intense focus on how organisations can keep reviewing and improving their efficiency and productivity on a regular basis. As always, there is a balance to be struck between the extremes of rational efficiency and the need to remain agile and have an eye to the need for contingencies.

In practice

Succeeding with kaizen

Kaizen starts with a fundamental and simple belief: all mistakes are to be eliminated, and if they do occur, they are to be studied and understood so they can be prevented from happening again. This requires a tireless commitment to the value of kaizen, coupled with several practical steps.

- Encourage people who carry out a task or activity to suggest improvements.
- Aim for gradual and continual improvements as opposed to large-scale changes.
- Make full use of data and other appropriate measures to assess the situation.
- Create formal feedback structures such as kaizen groups to ensure continuous dialogue and review.

Kaizen does, of course, have its own challenges and limitations. Its total approach can overshadow the potential contribution of much-needed experts. Individuals can struggle with the sustained pressure of constantly thinking of ways to improve. However, with the right balance of support and challenge to make sure that pressure does not become stress, involving people in doing things better can be enabling and engaging.

Re-engineering business processes

Anyone planning a re-engineering process will encounter four sequential phases:

- preparation
- process innovation and design
- implementation
- assessment.

Success depends on working through each stage in depth, making the most of diverse input, practical engagement and a range of ideas and support.

Phase 1. Preparation

Key tasks at this first stage include defining objectives, training and developing the team, mapping the overall process model (including sub-processes), defining customer needs, understanding the needs of the business, outlining potential breakthroughs and areas on which to focus, and preparing objectives.

Phase 2. Process innovation and design

This stage focuses on how processes and the work of the organisation can be improved or reinvigorated. It benefits from bold, radical thinking and covers several activities: visioning; using technology to improve working practices, efficiency and to reduce costs; cost–benefit analysis; communicating, engaging and preparing the organisation for change; and planning implementation.

Phase 3. Implementation

Making the changes work in practice involves piloting proposed changes; setting objectives for the implementation process; and training and mobilising people to achieve the desired goals.

Phase 4. Assessment

This phase is concerned with making adjustments and emphasises the vital importance of consolidation – holding the gains so that they become embedded in an organisation or team.

Many surgical teams routinely review all aspects of their work after each procedure; military units assess their successes as well as actual and potential weaknesses after an exercise or deployment; and process-heavy industries such as automotive manufacturing and construction periodically review their performance, with a view to making useful adjustments.

But the thinking that underpins BPR might just as easily be applied to a simple review of a presentation or pitch meeting, reviewing what you were trying to achieve, what went well and what could be improved and amended in future.

Thought starters

- What is your current process for improvement?
- Would your organisation benefit from gradual changes in the way you work, or from more radical and comprehensive rethinking?
- What processes cause the most frustration?
- What can you learn from other organisations?
- Who are the people in your organisation who have the greatest desire to change and improve? What can you do to help them?

What next?

Read *The Essential Deming: Leadership Principles from the Father of Quality* by Edwards Deming.

24

Systems thinking and the critical path

Understanding complex systems and their interactions

The big picture

Systems thinking is a way of viewing an organisation as part of a system with inputs and outputs that might include functions, supply chains and customers. It explores the relationships and connections between different components within a system, rather than focusing on individual constituent parts. Systems thinking demonstrates how a change in one part of a system can affect other parts of the system, and how the system can evolve over time.

The critical path is a method used to identify the most important tasks or activities in a process and to determine the most efficient route to complete that process. It involves mapping out all the tasks that need to be completed and identifying the dependencies between them (ie, the order in which things need to happen). By focusing on the critical path, organisations can identify the most important tasks and allocate resources to them accordingly.

Combining systems thinking and the critical path can help you to understand complex relationships and dependencies; it's all about making the most of resources and processes to achieve goals more effectively. It can also help to anticipate and mitigate potential risks, and to adapt to changing circumstances.

Systems thinking and the critical path can also be used to analyse and optimise complex business operations, such as supply chain management, manufacturing and customer service. This understanding can be used to improve organisational structures and shape culture, as well as identifying and addressing bottlenecks or inefficiencies.

About the ideas

There are six key elements of systems thinking.

1. *A holistic perspective.* Consider the whole system and how its various parts and elements interact with each other.

2. *Feedback loops.* Understand feedback loops within a system and their influence on its behaviour and evolution. Feedback loops are based on cause and effect. For example, a change in the way in which customer service calls are handled might result in a feedback loop of reduced or increased secondary calls to the same service centre.

3. *Emergence.* Recognise that complex systems can exhibit emergent behaviour, so the behaviour of the whole system is not necessarily predictable from the behaviour of its individual parts. This is an abstract concept, but it can be applied, for example, to financial markets where one company's financial results can positively or negatively affect an entire sector's performance. In extreme cases, poor performance may result in a behaviour to sell shares across all sectors, creating a crash.

4. *Interdependent relationships.* Understand the relationships between different parts of a system and how a change in one part can affect the rest of the system – for example, in complex supply chains that are moving to more sustainable ways of working. The ambition for one element within the system has an impact on the whole system.

5. *Dynamic behaviour.* Understand that systems can change and evolve over time in response to external and internal influences.

6. *Different perspectives.* Consider different perspectives and viewpoints to gain a more complete understanding of a system.

The critical path method involves several steps.

- *Identify tasks.* The first step in the critical path method is to identify all the tasks that need to be completed in order to achieve the goals or outcome desired.
- *Estimate duration.* The next step is to estimate the duration of each task, taking into account any dependencies or constraints that may affect the timeline.
- *Sequence tasks.* The third step is to sequence the tasks in the order they need to be completed, based on their dependencies and constraints.
- *Identify the critical path.* Then find the longest sequence of tasks and take into account the time required for each task, which gives you a total duration.
- *Monitor progress.* Finally, monitor progress, paying particular attention to tasks on the critical path. If any tasks on the critical path are delayed, it can affect the overall timeline.

The critical path helps you to consider the process of achieving an outcome and calculate the time required. Systems thinking allows you to consider the potential impact to the critical path in the event of changes within the system.

Systems thinking and the critical path are often associated with large-scale processes or projects where the (not insubstantial) task of identifying the relevant components of a system and understanding how they interact with each other is deemed worthwhile. There is also a danger that focusing on the system risks downplays other key factors, such as the wider competitive environment, or that the process may not be agile enough for fast-changing situations. But the ideas can still act as useful diagnostic and planning tools that provide data and insights to improve efficiency and highlight risks, whatever the size or type of your organisation.

In practice

If you're struggling to identify why a process or project is not as smooth or streamlined as you'd like, it might be worth giving the ideas a try. Here are some thoughts.

What are you looking to analyse or improve?

Clearly define the system or project that you want to analyse or optimise. This may involve identifying the goals or objectives of the system or project, and the stakeholders who are involved.

Map out the system or project

Create a map or diagram of the system or project, showing the relationships and dependencies between the different parts or components. This may involve identifying inputs, outputs, feedback loops and other elements of the system.

Analyse the system or project

Once you have a map of the system or project, you can use systems thinking techniques to analyse how it works and identify potential areas for improvement. This may involve looking for feedback loops, emergent behaviour and other characteristics of the system.

Identify the critical path

Use the critical path method to identify the tasks or activities that need to be completed in order to achieve your goals. You should also estimate the duration of each task and put them in the order they need to be completed, based on their dependencies and constraints.

Monitor progress

Once you have identified the critical path, you can use it to monitor progress. This may involve regularly reviewing the status of tasks on the critical path and making adjustments as needed.

Thought starters

- What are the goals or objectives of the system/project on which you are working?
- What are the main components or elements of the system or project? How do they interact with each other?
- What are the long-term implications of actions within the system or project? How can you ensure that you are making sustainable decisions?
- What are the most important tasks or activities in the project? How do they fit into the overall critical path?
- How can you adapt to changing circumstances and continue to optimise the system or project over time?

What next?

Read *Thinking in Systems* by Donella Meadows.

25

The balanced scorecard

Establishing the vital link between measuring and managing

The big picture

The balanced scorecard was devised in the 1990s by Robert Kaplan and David Norton. It was a response to the accelerating pace of change in society and, in particular, changing business models. Kaplan and Norton showed how managers can help people improve performance, achieve strategic objectives and increase the long-term value of their business by using a measurement and management system called the balanced scorecard. Their work contributed to greater focus on the benefits of measurement and metrics in organisations.

Central to Kaplan and Norton's approach is the belief that managers in businesses need to look beyond financial performance to remain competitive. They also believed that people prioritise and respond to those areas of their work that are being measured. They felt that companies that focus solely on financial issues were taking a restrictive, narrow view of their performance and ignored other areas that ultimately contributed to profitability but could not be measured in terms of revenue. For example, customer satisfaction or employee engagement do not contribute directly to financial measures like return on investment or earnings per share, but they are still important measures of success, particularly over the long term.

The framework injects rigour and, when used across teams or groups of people, consistency to the practical tasks of setting goals and focusing an individual's work. It can be used to break down goals and objectives into an action plan, with progress regularly assessed. This presents a comprehensive, relevant and balanced picture (hence the name) and highlights specific activities that need to be completed.

About the idea

The balanced scorecard (BSC) is a framework that helps managers to set goals and measure performance against them in four essential areas, with traditional "hard" financial measures forming only one of four quadrants. The other three more qualitative, operational measures are:

· the customer perspective: how a company is perceived by current and potential customers

· the internal perspective: those issues in which the company must excel

· the innovation and learning perspective: areas where a company must continue to improve and add value.

The BSC helps people to quickly gain a comprehensive perspective of the most significant issues affecting performance, including the various activities, priorities and skills needed to achieve their goals. It can also be used to identify areas where improvement or investment is required, and to create and implement a more targeted strategy.

It is valued as an effective tool for managing people through times of change, helping organisations to align their wider strategic goals with departmental and personal objectives. As a result, everyone understands what they need to do to achieve success, and how their work contributes to the success of the wider organisation – often a motivator for people

There's a reason why more quantifiable financial measures are so seductive. It's all too easy to misinterpret more qualitative measures; it's harder to set qualitative goals that measure the right things, that are clearly understood and don't drive unintended consequences and behaviours.

Clearly, a great deal of thought needs to go into what is measured, why and how. But, as a tool for encouraging people and organisations to go beyond strictly financial measures, BSC is a reminder of the importance of viewing and assessing performance more holistically. For example, it might take time for a senior leadership team to identify key metrics and measures but, once these are in place, they can be used to inform goal-setting throughout the business, keeping people broadly focused on the same areas while allowing for individual roles and abilities.

In practice

The BSC can be used at all levels within an organisation and in a range of contexts. For example, financial metrics for a sales team might include its spending budget, administrative costs or salaries bill; it isn't just about sales. Customers might also be internal: an IT department might measure the quality of its service levels to colleagues, for example.

Imagine that you are a leader of a functional team. To set goals for the team using the balanced scorecard, work through the following steps.

Start with the strategy

What are you trying to achieve? The first requirement is to define and communicate your strategy clearly. People need to understand wider strategic objectives or goals, the critical success factors that will help to achieve each objective or goal and how they can contribute.

Key questions at this stage include: what is the strategy? What are the strategic priorities? What do people need to do more, differently or better to progress the strategy? What are the guiding principles and shifts in thinking needed?

Decide what to measure

Goals and measures should be identified for each of the four perspectives that are relevant to the function, department or individual. Examples for each are included in Tables 3–6.

Key questions at this stage include: what are the most significant goals for each perspective? How will progress toward achieving these goals be measured?

TABLE 3: BALANCED SCORECARD: FINANCIAL PERSPECTIVE

Financial perspective

These include traditional financial indicators (such as sales and revenue, cost management, profitability), and should measure your progress toward your strategic goals.
They should provide shareholders and senior executives with the information they need to make informed decisions.

Goals	Measures
· Increased profitability	Cash flows
· Share price performance	Cost reduction
· Increased return on assets	Gross margins
	Return on capital/ equity/ investments/ sales
	Revenue growth
	Payment terms

TABLE 4: BALANCED SCORECARD: CUSTOMER PERSPECTIVE

Customers

Organisations first need to think carefully about what market segment they are supplying, and then set specific goals that relate to their current and potential customers.

Goals	Measures
· New customer acquisition	· Market share
· Customer retention	· Customer satisfaction
· Customer satisfaction	· Number of customers
· Cross-sales volumes	· Customer profitability
· Profit per customer.	· Delivery times
· Customer acquisition costs	· Units sold

TABLE 5: BALANCED SCORECARD: INTERNAL PROCESSES PERSPECTIVE

Internal processes

Consider your business processes, and what can be done to improve them and make them as efficient as possible.

Goals	Measures
• Improved core competencies	• Efficiency improvements
• Improved critical technologies	• Improved lead times
• Streamlined processes	• Reduced unit costs
• Improved employee morale	• Reduced waste
	• Improved sourcing/supplier delivery
	• Greater employee morale and satisfaction
	• Reduced staff turnover
	• Internal audit standards
	• Sales per employee

TABLE 6: BALANCED SCORECARD: INNOVATION AND LEARNING PERSPECTIVE

Innovation and learning

Given that people provide a foundation for vital tasks such as innovation and continuous improvement, it is valuable to set goals relating to employee development, retention and training.

Goals	Measures
• New product development	• Number of employees receiving training
• Continuous improvement	• Time needed to develop the next generation
• Employees' training and skills	• Percentage of products delivering 80% of sales revenue
	• Number of new products brought to market compared with the competition

Agree and implement the scorecards

Discuss and agree how the goals can be achieved and how progress and performance can be measured.

Key questions at this stage include: how will the goals and activities be agreed and communicated? How will people know what progress is being made?

The balanced scorecard

Develop performance measurement reviews

Once the balanced scorecard goals have been set and agreed, you need to measure and monitor progress towards achieving them.

Key questions include: how frequently will scorecards at individual and team level be assessed? How will insights and feedback across the organisation about progress be shared?

Plan and implement initiatives, generating momentum

Next, set clear objectives in each of the four areas (financial, customers, internal processes, learning and development) for each member of the team. These should be simple, achievable and practical, and reflect the overall objectives for the organisation.

Publicise and use the results

Everyone should understand the overall objectives, but deciding who should receive specific information, why and how often, is also important. Too much detail can lead to paralysis by analysis; too little and the benefits are lost. Use the information to guide decisions, strengthening areas that need further action and using the process dynamically.

Review and revise the system regularly

This allows wrinkles to be smoothed out and new or different goals to be set. The best way to tell if the balanced scorecard is working for your organisation is to set effective measurement goals every year and continue to meet them.

Thought starters

- How might you benefit from scorecards aligned with strategic priorities?
- Which aspects of your vision or plan could be enhanced and accelerated by adopting a balanced scorecard approach?

- How effectively are your performance goals set, measured and reviewed?
- How would you measure success for finance, customers, internal processes, innovation and learning for yourself, your team or department?
- How could adopting a BSC approach improve performance management for you and your colleagues?

What next?

Visit the Balanced Scorecard Institute website: www.balancedscorecard.org

26

Doblin's *Ten Types of Innovation*

Highlighting broad and comprehensive approaches to innovation

The big picture

When people think about innovation, they often think about ground-breaking new products and services plucked from the air by a lone genius prone to "Eureka!" moments. The truth is that such moments are rare, and that innovation is much more likely to be the product of teams of people thinking systematically about approaches and initiatives that solve a range of problems.

This broader concept of innovation is at the heart of the Doblin ten types of innovation framework developed by the consultancy Doblin to help organisations pursue multiple paths for driving growth and sustainability. The framework was introduced in the late 1990s and came to prominence in 2013 when Larry Keeley, one of Doblin's founders, published *Ten Types of Innovation*. Doblin itself is now part of Deloitte's Innovation Practice where the framework is used to help clients innovate.

The approach is based on the belief that, by considering a range of different types of innovation, organisations can identify opportunities for change and find creative solutions to address them. The ten types of innovation can be used to address a variety of business challenges, such as increasing competitiveness, improving customer satisfaction and driving growth.

About the idea

In the 1940s the economist Joseph Schumpeter coined the term "creative destruction" to describe the need for organisations to regularly destroy their own models of working to sustain competitive advantage over the long term. Doblin's model can be seen as a way of delivering Schumpeter's creative destruction concept across ten areas where organisations can focus to drive innovation.

1. *Performance*: improving the effectiveness or efficiency of a product or service.
2. *Product*: introducing new or improved products or services.
3. *Service*: introducing new or improved ways of delivering services to customers.
4. *Business model*: changing the way a company creates, delivers and captures value.
5. *Platform*: creating a foundation that enables other products or services to be built on top of it.
6. *Ecosystem*: creating and managing a network of partners and external stakeholders to create value.
7. *Customer experience*: enhancing the way customers interact with a company or brand.
8. *Brand*: building and maintaining a strong and distinct brand identity.
9. *Process*: improving the way an organisation operates internally.
10. *Enabling technology*: introducing new or improved technologies that enable other innovations.

By using this framework and identifying the key points of focus for improvement and enhancement, companies can develop their effectiveness in vital aspects of innovation, such as conducting research, gathering customer feedback, prototyping and testing new ideas, and implementing changes to products, services, processes or operating models.

The framework can be applied to a variety of organisational challenges and contexts and can be used to drive innovation in different areas of a company. It's a kind of mix and match menu of options to help identify the different ways in which companies can innovate.

It reminds you that innovation is not just about market-disrupting new products; it's also about being creative with supply chains and processes, business models and networks.

In addition to the ten types of innovation, Larry Keeley defined innovation ambition.

- *Core innovation*: incrementally changing what is already known as an existing process.
- *Adjacent innovation*: focusing on changing the boundaries to develop new capabilities, products and services that are close to what you already have.
- *Transformational innovation*: which is disruptive and creates something entirely new.

The strength of Doblin's approach is that it provides a high-level overview of different areas of innovation. That is also, of course, a potential weakness, with critics suggesting that such a broad-based approach fails to capture the complexity and nuance of specific situations, cultures and contexts. Neither does it offer specific guidance on how to prioritise between the different types of innovation on offer.

The following alternative frameworks and approaches for driving innovation are also worth considering.

Design thinking emphasises empathy, experimentation and iteration in the process of developing new ideas and solutions. It involves understanding the needs and perspectives of users, prototyping and testing ideas, and refining solutions based on feedback.

Lean approaches focuses on rapidly prototyping and testing new ideas to validate assumptions and learn from customer feedback. The goal is to identify and pursue the most promising ideas while minimising waste and risk.

Agile, an approach that originated in software development, can also be applied to other types of innovation. Agile emphasises flexibility, collaboration (between colleagues and with customers), and continuous iteration in the development process. Teams work in short cycles or "sprints" to deliver small increments of value and adapt quickly to changing conditions.

See also the topic of disruptive innovation, which is covered in Chapter 27.

Each of these approaches has its own strengths and limitations, and you may choose to use one or a combination of them depending on specific needs and goals.

Like all these approaches, Doblin's ten types of innovation is a valuable tool for thinking about innovation, a helpful building block to be used in conjunction with other tools and approaches that can help you to make sense of innovation depending on your specific context and business needs.

In practice

The ten distinct dimensions of the Doblin framework are a useful guide that can help you to identify, develop and implement innovative ideas. These ten types encompass both incremental and disruptive innovations, allowing businesses to explore a wide range of possibilities to drive growth and stay competitive in their markets.

Applying the framework effectively involves several steps.

Identify a business challenge or opportunity

Start by identifying an area where the company wants to drive change or innovation. This could be a problem that needs to be solved, a new market to be entered, or an opportunity to improve existing products or services.

Review the ten types of innovation

Consider each of the approaches to innovation and decide which ones are relevant to the challenge or opportunity identified. Think about how each type of innovation could be used to create value for customers, stakeholders or the company itself.

Significantly, these first two first steps are interchangeable.

The choice is either to focus first on where the greatest need for innovation lies by identifying a challenge or opportunity, or you may prefer to start by reviewing the ten types of innovation and identifying the one that would work best in your context.

Select the most promising types of innovation

Prioritise the types of innovation that promise the biggest impact and are most aligned with the company's goals and resources.

Gather data and insights

Explore the identified challenge or opportunity, including customer needs and preferences, market trends and the competitive landscape. This information can help inform and refine your approach.

Develop and test ideas

Use the data and insights gathered to develop and test ideas for addressing the challenge or opportunity. This may involve prototyping and testing different concepts, gathering feedback from customers and stakeholders, and iterating on the ideas.

Implement and scale

Once the most promising ideas have been identified, develop a plan for implementing and scaling them. This may involve making changes to products, services, processes or business models, and allocating resources to support the implementation.

Remember that the process of innovation is often iterative and may involve adapting and refining ideas based on feedback and balancing the need to refine existing products and services while developing new ones.

Thought starters

- What is the biggest business challenge or opportunity that you would like to address? Does it relate to performance, process, product, service or business model?

- What are the biggest pain points or challenges encountered by customers, and how will you fix them?
- Which of the ten types of innovation are most relevant for you?
- What foundation or platform is needed for your innovation to succeed over the long term?
- Who else can you involve in the vital activities of gathering data, developing and testing ideas, and implementing the innovation?

What next?

Read *Ten Types of Innovation: The Discipline of Building Breakthroughs* by Larry Keeley et al.

27

Disruptive innovation

Disrupting the status quo for substantive change

The big picture

Disruptive innovation is a theory of technological change developed by management thinker Clayton Christensen. Christensen wanted to understand why large and profitable companies – despite their wealth of resources – so often failed to capitalise on their success. For example, IBM's early computing innovations should logically have made it well placed to make the shift from mainframe to desktop to cloud computing. But it did not. Why didn't Ford think of Uber; one of the big hotel chains start up Airbnb; Kodak press home its advantage in digital photography?

The answer is that they were blindsided by new and nimbler *disruptors*.

In Christensen's view, disruptive innovations came from two types of market opportunity that are often overlooked by incumbents: low-end market footholds, and new-market footholds.

Low-end market footholds exist because incumbents typically focus on their most profitable and demanding customers, providing them with ever-improved products and services. In this situation a new entrant will typically offer a lower-cost and simpler product or service.

New-market footholds are less common: they are when a disrupter creates a market where none previously existed. As a result, they can be extremely profitable.

Disruptive innovation can have a significant impact on established industries and businesses, as it challenges existing norms and beliefs, and shifts the balance of power within a market. It can lead to the emergence of new business models, the introduction of new technologies, and the creation of entirely new markets. In some ways it is reminiscent of the bold, radical thinking of Chan Kim and Renee Mauborgne's blue ocean strategy.

About the idea

Christensen identified that most organisations understand and put into practice what he called *sustaining innovation*. This involves the development of new products or services that improve upon existing ones, but do not fundamentally change the way that a market operates. Sustaining innovations are often developed by established firms and are aimed at improving the performance of their products or services for their existing customers. They are an important, often crucial means of retaining and extending market share. But, for Christensen, the gradualism of sustaining innovation was under pressure from what he saw as an increasingly common pattern: disruptive innovation, which itself takes two main forms.

Low-end disruptive innovation

Disruptive innovation focusing on low-end markets involves the introduction of a new product or service that initially targets a small group of underserved or neglected customers, but eventually disrupts the market and challenges established products and organisations. This process often starts with the development of a simpler, cheaper and more convenient product or service that meets the needs of a specific group of consumers. As the disruptive entrant's product or service improves and becomes more appealing to a wider range of customers, it begins to capture market share from established firms.

A classic example of this type of disruptive innovation is provided by low-cost airlines. Traditionally, the airline industry focused on high-end customers, business flyers and regular customers. Airline companies introduced loyalty schemes and worked to improve everything from departure lounges to in-flight catering, comfort and entertainment. The millions of customers who simply wanted a cheaper service or were happy to accept a "no frills" approach was ignored, until the arrival of Southwest Airlines in the US, easyJet in Europe, and others who addressed these unmet needs.

New-market disruptive innovation

New-market footholds are scarcer and are often reliant on technological advances. This type of disruptive innovation occurs when disrupters create a new market where none had previously existed. In effect, they find a way to turn non-consumers into consumers.

A classic example is the iPod and iTunes music store which in the early 2000s changed the way consumers purchased and listened to music, transforming the music sales market and forcing many traditional retailers to shut their doors. The simplicity of the Apple iPod rapidly created an emerging market for digital music players. The iPod worked hand in glove with the iTunes music store, targeting the low-end music-buyer market and offering customers the ability to buy single music tracks rather than whole albums, which was how the incumbents primarily sold music.

Ultimately, disruptive innovation has the potential to fundamentally change the way that a market operates. Over time, the disruptive entrant's product or service may improve and become more appealing to a wider range of customers. As this occurs, the entrant begins to capture market share from the established firms, ultimately disrupting the market and changing the way that it operates.

The idea of "disruption" is a seductive one that has entered the business lexicon. But it's also often misunderstood. It's not simply a matter of "disrupt or be disrupted": a focus on supposedly disruptive technologies brings with it the danger of ignoring the role played by other factors such as a company's internal resources and capabilities in determining success. Market dynamics, organisational culture and the regulatory environment will also determine whether disruptive innovation is an appropriate approach for a specific organisation or sector.

Incumbents have also developed a range of strategies, such as acquiring disruptive start-ups or adapting their own business models to better meet the needs of their customers. (See Chapter 13, which addresses the topic of ambidexterity.)

Other theories of innovation

Several alternative theories of technological change and innovation sit alongside Christensen's theory of disruptive innovation.

Incremental innovation, like Christensen's idea of sustaining innovation, involves the step-by-step improvement of existing products or processes. Incremental innovation is often seen as a more gradual and less risky approach, as it involves building upon existing technologies and knowledge.

Archaic innovation involves the revival or reapplication of old or forgotten technologies or practices. Archaic innovations can be seen as a form of disruptive innovation, as they challenge the established ways of doing things and may disrupt existing markets. An interesting example is the return in popularity of vinyl records. These had almost vanished as a result of the rise of CDs in the 1980s and 1990s and music streaming services in the 2000s. However, the sound, equipment and process of owning and playing vinyl records is, for some, a nostalgic pastime, whereas for others it is simply pleasurable and fun. For record companies it is another, higher-margin format for the sale of new music as well as old.

In practice

The essence of disruptive innovation lies in transforming industries through new ideas and approaches, often starting with a niche market and gradually displacing established incumbents.

Here are a few steps you can use to assess whether Christensen's theory of disruptive innovation – or aspects of it – might work for you and your organisation.

Identify underserved or neglected customer segments

Disruptive innovation starts by targeting customers who are not served well by existing products or services. You can look for opportunities to serve these customers by offering a simpler, cheaper or more convenient solution.

Continue building with continuous improvement

As your disruptive product or service improves, it can begin to appeal to a wider range of customers. You can then use customer feedback and data to continuously improve the product or service, making it more appealing to mainstream customers.

Develop a low-end or new-market foothold

Disruptive innovations often start by targeting a small group of customers with a basic or stripped-down version of the product or service. This enables you to establish a foothold in the market and gather feedback from customers. The early days of a website called "The Facebook" (now just Facebook, owned by Meta) is an interesting example, with the platform initially targeting American university students – people similar to "The Facebook's" co-founders such as Mark Zuckerberg.

Expand into adjacent markets

As the disruptive innovation gains traction, you can look for opportunities to expand into adjacent markets or industries. This can help to disrupt the market further and capture more market share. For example, Uber moved from delivering people to their destination to the adjacent market of delivering food.

Adapt to changing market conditions

Markets are constantly changing, and you need to be prepared to adapt to new developments. This may involve adjusting the product or service offering, adopting new business models, or entering into new partnerships or collaborations. Numerous players entered the low-cost airline market but not all were able to survive with such low margins. The market now has fewer, more established low-cost operators.

Thought starters

- Think about the market you operate in and consider how it could be transformed by a disruptor.
- Do you have a product or service that can create a new market?
- What customers are currently being under-served or neglected?
- How can new technology create new products or services and open up new markets in your industry?
- What could you do to anticipate and respond to potential disruptive innovations in your market?

What next?

Read *The Innovator's Dilemma: When New Technologies Cause Great Firms to Fail* by Clayton Christensen.

28

The growth share matrix

A popular way to view business potential and growth

The big picture

The growth share matrix (originally known as the BCG matrix) is used to evaluate the relative market position of a company's business units or products. It helps businesses identify which areas of their business are generating the most cash, which will continue to generate cash in the future, and which areas are draining cash.

Originally developed by Alan Zakon and colleagues working at the Boston Consulting Group (BCG), the matrix was popularised in 1970 by BCG's founder, Bruce Henderson, in an essay entitled "The product portfolio". The growth share matrix was preceded by the development of a range of strategic management concepts and tools, including the Ansoff matrix, as well as the work of Peter Drucker and Michael Porter's five forces framework. These laid the foundations for the emergence of strategic management as a distinct discipline, which influenced the creation of the growth share matrix.

About the idea

The growth share matrix is based on two dimensions: market growth and market share.

Market growth refers to the rate at which the market for a particular product or service is growing, while market share refers to the percentage of total sales that a company has in a particular market.

The growth share matrix is used widely to prioritise efforts and to allocate resources. It helps businesses to focus on their strengths and manage their weaknesses, and it can be used to identify opportunities for growth and diversification.

The growth share matrix involves plotting a company's products or business units on a grid with the *x*-axis representing market share, and the *y*-axis representing market growth.

The matrix consists of four quadrants, as shown in Figure 5.

1. *Stars*: products or business units that have a high market share in a rapidly growing market. They require significant investment to maintain their position, but have the potential to generate large amounts of cash in the future.
2. *Cash cows*: products or business units that have a high market share in a mature market. They generate significant amounts of cash, but have low or limited growth potential.

Figure 5: **The BCG Matrix**

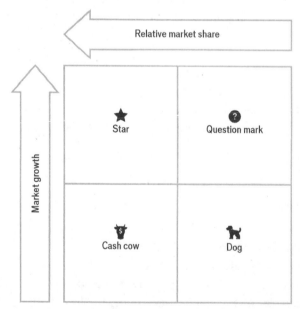

Source: Boston Consulting Group

3. *Dogs*: products or business units that have a low market share in a mature market. They do not generate much cash and have low growth potential.

4. *Question marks*: products or business units that have a low market share in a rapidly growing market. They may have the potential to become stars, but they also have a high risk of failure and require significant investment and effort to grow.

The growth share matrix is a popular tool because it provides a simple and intuitive framework for evaluating the market position of products or business units. But it is also important to understand its limitations and consider other factors when making strategic decisions. It can be used alongside other tools including SWOT and PEST analysis and Porter's five forces model to achieve a more balanced and holistic picture.

As with any framework or model, there are concerns that the growth share matrix oversimplifies market conditions and ignores external factors that may affect a company's performance. It also takes little account of the different costs and resources required to support different products or business units. And as it is based on historical data, it may not predict future market conditions accurately. Its contemporary relevance for a fast-moving and unpredictable business environment has also been questioned, although the Boston Consulting Group continues to update guidance on how it can best be used, suggesting that since its inception, companies tend to cycle through the quadrants more quickly and may need to experiment more by focusing more on question marks than they might have in the past.

In practice

With these caveats in mind, the growth share matrix provides a framework for analysing a company's portfolio of products based on their market growth rate and relative market share, enabling strategic decision-making about resource allocation and growth potential.

To apply the growth share matrix in your own context, follow these steps.

Identify what you want to analyse

This could be individual or groups of products or services or a business division or function.

Gather data

Collect relevant data for each product or business unit, including market size and relative market share. This data can be obtained through market research, sales figures, market reports and competitive analysis.

Calculate market growth rate

Assess the market growth rate for each product or business unit. This involves evaluating the annual growth rate of the market in which the product operates. This information can be obtained by analysing market trends, industry reports and historical data.

Determine relative market share

Calculate the relative market share of each product or business unit by dividing your product's market share by the market share of your largest competitor. Market share data can be obtained from sales figures, market research and industry reports.

Plot the products/business units

Create a matrix with two axes, one representing market growth rate and the other representing relative market share. Plot each product or business unit on the matrix based on their respective market growth rate and relative market share values.

Interpret the matrix categories

Analyse the position of each product or business unit on the matrix and categorise them accordingly, so you can develop strategies to deal with them.

- *Stars.* Allocate resources and investments to support the growth of stars and maintain their market dominance.

- *Cash cows*. Maximise profitability and cash flow from cash cows. Reinvest the generated cash into stars or question marks to foster growth.
- *Dogs*. Evaluate the performance and potential of dogs. Consider divestment or restructuring if necessary or explore ways to turn them into question marks or stars.
- *Question marks*. Conduct market research, invest selectively, and develop strategies to convert question marks into stars or consider divestment if they don't show potential.

Monitor and adjust

Review the growth share matrix regularly and reassess the position of products or business units as market conditions change. Keep track of market growth rates, relative market share and overall performance to make informed decisions about resource allocation and strategic focus.

Thought starters

- How do the market growth rate and market share of each of your products or business units compare with those of your competitors?
- What strengths and weaknesses of your products or business units are affecting their market position?
- What is the best way to allocate resources to maximise the return on investment for each product?
- Are there any products or business units that are in a "question mark" phase, with the potential to become stars or dogs?
- How can you use the growth share matrix with other tools to get a more comprehensive view of your market position?

What next?

Read the article "BCG classics revisited: the growth share matrix" by Martin Reeves, Sandy Moose and Thijs Venema.

29

Product life cycle model

From ideation to retirement – the product life cycle

The big picture

The business world is littered with tales of proud brands and products that once burned brightly but whose star has waned. Video cassettes were once at the cutting edge of home entertainment; now even DVDs have given way to streaming services. The photographic juggernaut that was Kodak is a shadow of its former self. Such rise and fall can seem like the inevitable ebb and flow of technological and societal change. But are there strategies that companies can use to understand these flows and perhaps delay or postpone seemingly inevitable decline?

The product life cycle (PLC) model is here to help. It's a framework used to describe the stages that a product or service passes through, from introduction to the market until its decline and eventual withdrawal.

Emerging as a popular marketing concept in the mid-1960s, the PLC model has since evolved as a way to understand the dynamics of products in their markets. It helps you to develop appropriate marketing strategies and maximise profits at each stage of a product's life cycle, anticipating and mitigating challenges, helping you to change direction and, if necessary, manage decline.

About the idea

The PLC model typically consists of four stages that define a product's life cycle: introduction, growth, maturity and decline.

Introduction

The introduction stage is where a new product is launched on the market. This stage is characterised by low sales volume, limited distribution, and high marketing and advertising costs. During this stage, organisations are focused on establishing a market for the product and creating a brand image that will resonate with customers. They will often offer introductory pricing or discounts to encourage early adoption and to gain a foothold in the market. An interesting example is provided by the introduction of electric vehicles (EVs). During the introduction stage, EVs were new and unfamiliar to most consumers, leading to organisations like Tesla focusing on raising awareness through marketing campaigns which showcased the EV benefits.

Growth

Growth is the second stage of the product life cycle model, during which sales of the product begin to increase, and organisations can start to realise profits. The growth stage is characterised by an increase in demand, expanding distribution channels and increased competition. Companies must also be prepared to respond to changing market conditions and customer preferences to ensure continued growth and profitability.

Smartphones, which experienced rapid growth as consumers adopted them, are an example of what can be achieved in the growth stage. Companies such as Apple and Samsung have invested heavily in marketing and product development, introducing new features to attract new customers, and to retain and build market share.

Maturity

Maturity is the third stage of the product life cycle model, during which sales growth begins to slow as the market becomes saturated, customer needs shift and competition increases. The maturity stage is characterised by intense competition, product differentiation and cost-cutting measures.

During the maturity stage, the focus is all about maintaining market share and maximising profits by optimising production processes, reducing costs and expanding into new markets. Investing in product differentiation will help products to stand out from competitors and maintain customer loyalty.

Breakfast cereals are an interesting example, where a market is saturated and sales have stabilised. Multiple brands offer a wide range of options and competition is intense. Companies focus on maintaining market share through price competition, promotion and brand loyalty. Product diversification helps to extend the product's life cycle.

Decline

Decline is the final stage of the product life cycle model, during which businesses or products may face increasing competition from newer products and technologies. It is characterised by falling sales, declining profits and reduced demand. During the decline stage, businesses must focus on managing the product's decline while maximising profitability. They may need to reduce production costs, liquidate stock and focus on more profitable customer segments. They may also need to invest in marketing and advertising to maintain awareness and generate continuing interest in the product.

The decline stage can be challenging, but it is also an opportunity to learn from past performance (especially mistakes) and identify new opportunities for growth and innovation. By carefully managing the decline stage and making key decisions – for example, how to extend the life of the product, what to do about pricing, how to look after existing clients, when to time the introduction of new offerings – businesses are better able to sustain their success and brand reputation in the long term.

An example is provided by the decline of DVD sales and rentals, resulting from the rise of streaming services and digitisation. As consumers shifted towards digital streaming platforms like Netflix, rental stores faced reduced sales and profitability, leading to store closures and a decline in the release of DVDs.

In practice

So how can you use the product life cycle model to understand the dynamics of your products or services in their market and develop appropriate marketing strategies to boost their success?

Here are some pointers.

Conduct market research

Accurately determine consumer demand, competition and trends in the market. This information can help you make informed decisions about product development, pricing and marketing strategies. Gather data on customer needs, emerging trends and competitor offerings.

Identify the stage of the PLC model that your product is in

This helps with decisions about how best to maximise profitability and prolong the product's life cycle so that you can make the most of your product at each stage.

Develop an appropriate marketing strategy

This needs to be based on the current stage of the PLC model and tailored to the product's current situation. You might consider adjusting pricing and distribution strategies to ensure that the product remains as competitive and profitable as possible. For example, during the growth stage, businesses may consider lowering prices to attract more customers, whereas during the decline stage, they may focus on selling off remaining inventory.

You could also offer competitive pricing or bundles, depending on the product, to attract certain customers or market segments.

Maximise the chances of success during the introduction phase

Consider strategies such as:

- targeting potential early adopters

- creating a unique selling proposition that differentiates their product from competitors in the market
- making sure that the product meets customer expectations and gathers positive reviews.

Monitor and adjust strategies

This may involve making changes to product features, pricing or marketing tactics to stay competitive and extend the product's life cycle.

Expand the focus

Once growth has started accelerating, focus on two issues simultaneously: meeting increased demand while also working to build brand loyalty and market share.

This may mean increasing production capacity, expanding distribution channels, and investing in marketing and advertising to continue to build awareness and generate interest in the product. This is an opportunity for businesses to establish a dominant position in the market and build a strong brand identity. They may offer new product features, improve product quality or expand product lines to appeal to a wider range of customers. Price competition may also become more intense during the growth stage, as new competitors enter the market and existing competitors work to maintain their market share.

Thought starters

- Consider a product or product lines that you're involved with. Which stage of the PLC model is that product in? What factors led you to this conclusion?
- What are your competitors doing at each stage of the PLC model? Are there any lessons you can learn from their successes or failures?

- How can you extend the life cycle of the product? What strategies might keep it in the growth stage or maturity stage for longer?
- Are there any emerging technologies or trends that may affect the life cycle of the product? How can you stay ahead of these changes?
- With the PLC in mind, how can you adjust your messaging and tactics to resonate better with your target audience?

What next?

Read *The Product Book: How to Become a Great Product Manager* by Josh Anon and Carlos González de Villaumbrosia.

30

Net Promoter Score

Knowing your customers and measuring their loyalty

The big picture

Net Promoter Score (NPS)® is a customer loyalty measurement tool that assesses the willingness of customers to recommend a company's products or services. It is based on the premise that customers who are more loyal to a company are more likely to recommend it to others.

Net Promoter Score is a proprietary tool developed in 2001 by Fred Reichheld, then a partner at Bain & Company in conjunction with Satmetrix. The tool started as a way of measuring how well an organisation treats and meets the needs of customers, leading to brand loyalty. Over the following decades it has been refined and improved to be used beyond just customers and is now also seen as a tool to measure employee engagement and loyalty.

The broad popularity and widespread use of NPS are attributed to its simplicity: the ease of implementation, with transparent methodology and clear results that highlight where changes need to be made. The simplicity of the NPS informed the creation of what is called the pulse survey, which is a widely used initiative for measuring everything from employee happiness through to understanding complex change programmes within companies.

About the idea

NPS is formulated by asking customers a single simple question. They are asked to rate their likelihood of recommending a company, product or service on a scale of 0 to 10, with 0 being not at all likely and 10 being extremely likely.

Customers who give a rating of 9 or 10 are considered *promoters*, those who give a rating of 7 or 8 are considered *passives*, and those who give a rating of 0 to 6 are considered *detractors*. NPS is calculated by subtracting the percentage of detractors from the percentage of promoters (see Figure 6).

For example, if a company has 50% promoters, 40% passives and 10% detractors, its NPS would be 50% − 10% = 40.

Scores can range from −100 (all respondents are detractors) to +100 (all respondents are promoters). A positive NPS indicates that a company has more promoters than detractors; a negative NPS indicates that a company has more detractors than promoters. NPS is typically expressed as a score between a minimum and maximum number rather than as a percentage.

In most cases, the single NPS question "How likely are you to recommend a company on a scale of 0 to 10?" is accompanied by open-ended questions to gain more insight. Examples include "Why have you given this response?" or "driver questions" designed to dig deeper and provide greater insight into certain aspects of the customer experience and journey. For example, a hotel customer may have been very satisfied until they reached the point of checkout, which was unsatisfactory.

NPS is often used as a key performance indicator (KPI) to gauge overall satisfaction and the loyalty of customers. It is believed to

Figure 6: **How the Net Promoter Score is calculated**

Promoters minus Detractors = Net Promoter Score

be a strong predictor of a company's growth and success, because customers who are more loyal tend to make more purchases, at higher prices, and are more likely to remain loyal over time. The tool (and any subsequent associated questions) can also be used to identify areas of dissatisfaction, improvement and growth, while tracking the success of customer initiatives.

NPS has also evolved as a metric of employee satisfaction, with the question for employee satisfaction slightly changed to read: "Would you recommend the company as a place of work?" As for customer satisfaction, the tool can be used to identify positive trends as well as areas of discontent and potential growth.

The simplicity of NPS is also a potential downside. Critics suggest that relying on a single question might provide clarity, but it cannot capture the wider range of factors that influence customer satisfaction and behaviour, such as product quality, convenience or value for money. As with any ratings system, your 9 out of 10 might not mean the same as someone else's 9 out of 10. The concept of loyalty might differ for each customer depending on their specific needs, which is evident in the food retail, airline and hotel sectors where loyalty to one brand is not uncommon. It's also true that self-reported data may not necessarily reflect actual behaviour: a score of 9 or 10 does not mean that a person will make a recommendation; only that, at the moment of being asked, that is how they felt.

In practice

NPS is a simple tool to apply, but there are several key steps in its use and application.

Determine your target audience

NPS is typically used to measure the loyalty and satisfaction of a company's customers or employees, so it is important to identify the specific group you want to survey.

Select your survey method

There are a few different ways to gather NPS data, including online surveys, telephone surveys and in-person surveys. Select the method that is most appropriate for the target audience.

Ask the NPS question

The standard NPS question is: "On a scale of 0 to 10, how likely are you to recommend [x] to a friend or colleague?" or: "How likely are you to recommend us to a friend or colleague?" You can also ask an open-ended follow-up question to gather more detailed feedback, such as: "What's the primary reason for your score?"

Calculate your NPS

To calculate the NPS of your company or product, divide your respondents into three groups: promoters (9 to 10), passives (7 to 8), and detractors (0 to 6). Calculate the percentage of respondents in each group, and then subtract the percentage of detractors from the percentage of promoters. This will give you the NPS, which can range from −100 (all respondents are detractors) to +100 (all respondents are promoters).

Analyse and act on your NPS data

Once you have your NPS, analyse the data to understand what is driving the score and identify areas for improvement. This may involve making changes to your products or services, improving the customer experience, or changing workplace systems and processes that are getting in the way of employee engagement. It is also important to track your NPS over time to monitor any changes and identify trends.

The objective of NPS is to increase the score over time using the data from each survey to make improvements. However, to use NPS effectively companies should conduct regular surveys of both customers and employees to track the impact (if any) of post-survey initiatives. Regular tracking and follow-up provides immediate insight into satisfaction levels which, if they are declining over time, might trigger the need for a more in-depth analysis to understand where to focus and what to change.

Thought starters

- Would implementing the Net Promoter Score system in your company be beneficial? If so, in what ways?
- If you already have high satisfaction levels, how can you use this information to boost retention and loyalty further?
- How can you address the concerns and feedback from detractors to improve their experience and potentially convert them into promoters?
- Are there any specific patterns or trends in the responses of passives? How can you turn them into more engaged and satisfied customers or employees?
- How can you use the NPS data to identify areas for process improvement and make meaningful changes to your products or services?

What next?

Read *The Ultimate Question: Driving Good Profits and True Growth* by Fred Reichheld.

31

Kotler's four Ps of marketing

Creating a sound marketing strategy by focusing on four key elements

The big picture

Philip Kotler's four Ps of marketing is a framework first created and published in his 1967 book *Marketing Management: Analysis, Planning, Implementation and Control.* By focusing on four essential elements – product, price, place and promotion – Kotler believed that organisations could develop comprehensive marketing strategies that take into account the needs of the target market, the need for differentiation, the competitive landscape, and other external factors that may affect the success of the marketing effort.

Over the years since the four Ps were first introduced, they have been expanded and adapted to reflect the changing business environment as well as the emergence of new technologies and marketing channels. But the founding four Ps remain a relevant, foundational concept in the field of marketing.

About the idea

The four Ps of marketing provide a practical framework for designing and implementing marketing strategies.

Product

Product refers to the goods or services that a company offers. A product should be designed to meet the needs of the target market and should be differentiated from competitors. A well designed and differentiated product has the potential to attract and retain customers, increase sales and drive revenue growth.

Price

Price is the amount of money that a customer is willing to pay for a product or service. This is determined by factors such as production costs, competition and customer demand. By understanding the factors that influence pricing strategy, a company can set competitive and attractive prices while ensuring it maximises profitability.

Place

Place refers to the channels through which a product or service is distributed to customers. By focusing on the key elements of place (also known as distribution), companies can ensure that their products are available to customers when and where they need them. Effective distribution increases sales, improves customer satisfaction and builds brand loyalty.

Promotion

Promotion refers to activities that promote an organisation's products to customers. Promotion can include advertising, public relations, sales promotions and personal selling. By focusing on promotion, organisations can create effective marketing campaigns that reach their target audience and generate sales. A well-executed promotional campaign can help to build brand awareness, generate interest in a product or service, and drive business growth.

Since Kotler's model was first developed, the world of marketing has been transformed and several additional Ps have been proposed and added. These provide a broader perspective and address specific areas of focus in marketing.

Here are some of the commonly added Ps.

People: the focus on the people involved in the marketing process, including customers, employees and stakeholders, emphasising the importance of understanding and catering to their needs, preferences and behaviours.

Process: the series of activities and steps involved in delivering a product or service to customers, emphasising the efficiency and effectiveness of the processes involved in marketing, such as supply chain management, customer service and order fulfilment.

Partnerships: collaborations and alliances an organisation forms with other organisations to enhance marketing efforts, including strategic partnerships, joint ventures and other cooperative arrangements that help expand reach, access resources, leveraging complementary strengths.

Physical evidence: the tangible elements that contribute to the overall customer experience, including factors such as packaging, branding, store layout, and other physical cues that shape customer perceptions and interactions with a product or service.

Performance: the measurement and evaluation of marketing efforts, including metrics and key performance indicators to assess the effectiveness and efficiency of marketing campaigns, customer satisfaction, sales performance and overall business success.

Packaging: the specific focus on design and presentation of a product's packaging, while recognising the impact of packaging on customer perceptions, product differentiation and brand image.

The addition of these Ps is not universally accepted or standardised. Different experts have their perspectives, experiences and areas of focus. The number of Ps you choose to use will depend on your specific context – but the original four will still stand you in good stead whether you are making widgets or offering the latest AI-based tech service.

In practice

Kotler's four Ps model emphasises the importance of product, price, place and promotion in developing a comprehensive marketing strategy. It highlights the need to align these elements to meet customer needs, differentiate and create value for the target market.

Here are some thoughts on using the four Ps in practice, with a simple example.

Product

1. Determine the features, benefits and unique selling points of your product.
2. Conduct market research to understand customer needs and preferences.
3. Develop a product strategy that aligns with your target market and positioning.
4. Continuously improve and innovate your product based on customer feedback.

Price

1. Conduct pricing research to understand market dynamics and customer willingness to pay.
2. Set a pricing strategy that reflects the value of your product or service.
3. Consider factors such as production costs, competitor pricing and customer perceptions.
4. Offer pricing options such as discounts, bundles or premium pricing based on customer segments.

Place

1. Identify the most effective distribution channels to reach your target market.
2. Establish partnerships with retailers, distributors and online platforms.
3. Optimise logistics and supply chain management to ensure timely delivery.
4. Consider factors such as geographic reach, accessibility and convenience for customer segments.

Promotion

1. Develop a comprehensive marketing communication plan.

2. Determine the most suitable channels to reach your target audience (eg, social media, advertising, PR).
3. Create compelling messaging that highlights the unique benefits of your product.
4. Implement promotional activities such as advertising campaigns, content marketing or influencer partnerships.

Consider, for example, a small independent coffee shop opening in a new area.

Coffee shop: Product
- The shop offers a variety of specialty coffees, pastries and sandwiches.
- The shop ensures the quality of its products by sourcing fresh and locally roasted coffee beans and using high-quality ingredients.
- It differentiates itself by offering unique flavours and personalised customer preferences (eg, offering dairy-free alternatives, seasonal specials).

Coffee shop: Price
- The shop sets competitive prices based on market research and local competition.
- It offers different pricing options such as sizes (small, medium, large) and add-ons (eg, whipped cream, flavoured syrups).
- The shop periodically runs promotions or loyalty programmes to encourage repeat visits and customer loyalty.

Coffee shop: Place
- The shop is in a high-traffic area, easily accessible to both pedestrians and drivers.
- It has a comfortable and inviting ambiance, with ample seating and free Wi-Fi.

- It offers takeout and online ordering options to cater to customers on the go.

Coffee shop: Promotion

- The shop engages in local marketing efforts, such as distributing flyers in nearby offices and residences.
- It has a strong presence on social media platforms, sharing updates, specials and engaging with customers.
- It collaborates with local influencers, hosts events to attract new customers and creates buzz around the brand.

In this example, the four Ps model acts as a sort of checklist to make sure the coffee shop thinks about all aspects of these core elements of marketing: a quality product, appropriately priced, available in a convenient location, and effectively promoted to the target audience. This comprehensive approach will help the coffee shop to attract customers, differentiate itself from competitors and drive business growth.

Thought starters

- What are the four Ps of your products and services? Is there further scope to differentiate your product from competitors' offerings?
- What pricing strategies are most appropriate for your product or service?
- How can you effectively communicate the value of your product at the chosen price?
- How can you optimise the distribution process to ensure that your product is accessible and convenient for customers?
- What messaging and communication channels will resonate most with your target market?

What next?

Read *Marketing Management* by Philip Kotler et al.

32

Gladwell's tipping point

How ideas become viral

The big picture

The publication in 2000 of *The Tipping Point: How Little Things Can Make a Big Difference* by writer Malcom Gladwell was, fittingly, a publishing sensation.

In his debut work, Gladwell addressed a significant question through the prism of technological advance and globalisation: how does an idea spread far and fast? Gladwell's answers were to reshape marketing in the 21st century, as well as affecting issues as diverse as social policy, fashion, popular culture, politics and the development of social media. The notion that we can make an image or idea "go viral" owes much to the insights of Gladwell's tipping point.

Gladwell defines a "tipping point" as the moment when an idea, behaviour or product crosses a threshold and starts to spread rapidly. He uses the metaphor of a virus to represent an idea or trend: spreading slowly at first before rapidly becoming an infectious outbreak or epidemic.

About the idea

Malcolm Gladwell highlights three key reasons why certain ideas "tip" and spread virally.

Key people who play pivotal roles

First, he highlights the impact of a relatively few people who have pivotal roles.

Connectors bring people together and communicate across different networks. They may only have weak connections, but they are people who can spread ideas outside one specific group.

Mavens are also connectors, but they are typically more opinionated and focused on the needs of others. *Mavens* include people such as social media influencers, educators, journalists and commentators.

Salespeople "sell" the idea by merit of the trust that others have in them. For example, while he was US president, Bill Clinton mentioned in a press conference that he was enjoying *The Tipping Point*, a comment that immediately accelerated sales of the book.

The stickiness factor

The second force driving the spread of ideas and highlighted by Gladwell is the *stickiness factor*. This has two elements:

- the extent to which the product or idea is genuinely appealing and attractive
- the ability to rise above the clutter of other messages and similar ideas or products that happen to be around.

These two factors matter hugely. If something is unappealing or unoriginal it will be rejected, regardless of how well it is promoted.

The power of context

The final factor driving the rapid, viral spread of an idea is *the power of context*. Changes in context or priority can cause a message to "tip" and become an epidemic. This is because people's circumstances matter, so altering their environment – or even just promising to alter it – can result in an idea to tip.

In his book Gladwell explains the power of context by using the example of "broken windows theory": the notion that visible signs of anti-social behaviour and low-level crime (for example, vandalism and "broken windows") can lead to the spread of much more serious crime, because criminality is already being tolerated. This theory, which many people believe is a gross oversimplification, was used in New York in the 1990s by the police commissioner, William Bratton. The "zero tolerance" approach targeting minor crime, such as fare-dodging and vandalism, led to a large fall in crime overall.

In practice

How can you reach the tipping point with your idea, product or service? Gladwell suggests that several steps are needed to spread an idea "virally".

1. Choose a compelling, attractive proposition or idea to spread. Something interesting, unusual or potentially beneficial to a group of people.
2. Understand, in as much detail as possible, what makes the proposition or idea distinctive and compelling, and then highlight these issues.
3. Directly engage the three key types of people: those with connections and large networks ("connectors"); influencers ("mavens"), such as journalists; and people with influence ("salespeople"), such as celebrities or other "heroes".
4. Spread the idea at the right time, capitalising on the environment and making sure that the idea is relevant, timely and being spread on fertile ground.

Thought starters

- Which tipping points or viral ideas have impressed you recently? Why did they succeed?
- Which idea, product or concept could you spread using tipping point techniques?
- Are you one of the three types of people that are central to spreading ideas (connector, maven or salesperson)?
- What is the best way for you to communicate and develop "stickiness"? For example, is social media best – and, if so, which platform?

- How could you support something – a charity campaign, for example – using tipping point techniques?

What next?

Read *The Tipping Point: How Little Things Can Make a Big Difference* by Malcolm Gladwell.

33

Lewin's leadership styles

Making the most of different approaches to leadership

The big picture

Kurt Lewin was a psychologist and pioneer in the field of social psychology. In 1939, he led a group of researchers to understand the different styles that leaders use to influence their colleagues. The result of their work is now commonly referred to as "Lewin's leadership framework". At the time, much of the research on leadership had focused on the traits and characteristics of leaders, but Lewin argued that the more flexible concept of leadership styles, based on *how leaders behave*, was more important and accurate in determining how effective a leader would be.

Since Lewin's work, the concept of leadership styles and behaviour has been studied widely and is an important part of the field of leadership and management. Many researchers have refined and expanded upon Lewin's original framework (some are outlined below) but his basic ideas about the importance of leadership styles, defined by behaviour, and the need for leaders to adapt their style to meet the needs of their team remain influential.

About the idea

According to Lewin, there are three main leadership styles: authoritarian, democratic and laissez-faire. It is now widely recognised that the most effective leaders are those who use a combination of styles, varying their approach according to the

173

situation, team and task, and adapting to both the individuals being led and the tasks to be achieved.

Authoritarian leadership

Authoritarian leadership, also known as autocratic leadership, involves the leader making all the decisions and not involving others in the decision-making process. This style is often used in situations where quick decisions have to be made, but it can be seen as unresponsive to the needs and opinions of team members.

Authoritarian leadership might be on show in start-up businesses driven by entrepreneurs who are impatient to realise their vision, or in high-stakes situations, like surgery, in combat, or in an extreme crisis, where it would be too time consuming or impossible to consult or delegate. There are times when being more directive is important, but it is widely accepted these days that this leadership style should be used with caution.

Democratic leadership

Democratic leadership, also known as participative leadership, involves the leader engaging team members in the decision-making process and encouraging them to contribute their ideas and opinions. This style is often seen as more collaborative and can lead to higher levels of engagement and commitment among team members.

This is the style most routinely demonstrated in organisations today. From project teams to boards of directors and everything in between, teams generally rely on active participation, mutual support and democratic leadership. In most organisations, people expect to be able to express their view and contribute.

Laissez-faire leadership

Laissez-faire leadership, also known as delegative leadership, involves the leader providing minimal direction and allowing team members to make their own decisions. This style can be effective in situations where team members have the knowledge, experience and skills to make good decisions, but if they don't, it can lead to a lack of direction and a lack of accountability.

Laissez-faire leadership might be the default where roles are spread over a wide geographical area. It can work well where skill and experience levels allow, or when you're giving someone the chance to show what they can do. But it needs careful consideration and should not simply be the result of a leader being too "hands off" or defaulting to the style because of being overwhelmed or because of a lack of resources.

Most people would not recognise Lewin's world of work. Since the 1930s, it has changed beyond recognition, and thinking about leadership behaviours and styles has evolved accordingly. Lewin's styles have been criticised for being too simplistic and for lacking a proper appreciation of situation and context. But his focus on patterns of behaviour remains an underpinning for the many, more finessed frameworks that have evolved to help people make sense of the different styles that leaders might deploy and when.

Situational leadership emphasises the importance of adapting your leadership style to fit the needs and abilities of the team and the specific tasks being undertaken. According to this theory, there is no one-size-fits-all leadership style, and leaders should be flexible and adapt their approach to fit the needs of their team and the situation at hand (see Chapter 34).

Servant leadership focuses on the importance of serving the needs of the team and the organisation. Servant leaders place the needs of their followers ahead of their own and work to empower and develop their team members.

Authentic leadership suggests that leaders need to be genuine, transparent and self-aware. Authentic leaders are able to be vulnerable and open with their team and can build trust and credibility by being honest and transparent.

Transformational leadership focuses on inspiring and motivating followers to achieve their full potential. Transformational leaders create a shared vision and empower and challenge their followers to think creatively and take (calculated) risks to achieve it.

In practice

Lewin's leadership style framework and the theories that build on it suggest that to achieve the best results leaders should adapt their style to the situation they are facing and the skills, experience and attitude of the people they are working with. Most leaders have a preferred or default style but this may not always be the most appropriate.

For example, in a crisis, more direction might be appropriate. When the going is good and you want to develop colleagues, a more democratic style would work better. Leaders may also find themselves adopting different styles for different team members depending on the capability and experience they have for the task they are doing.

Here are a few tips for applying Kurt Lewin's leadership styles framework in practice.

Decide the most appropriate style for the situation

This will depend on the situation and the needs of the team. Consider the skills, knowledge and collective experience of the team, the complexity and significance of the task at hand, and the time available for decision-making.

Communicate clearly

Regardless of leadership style, it is important to communicate clearly with the team about expectations and the decision-making process. This will help to ensure that everyone is on the same page and is working together towards an agreed goal.

Be open to feedback

Allowing team members to provide feedback and input will help to create a more collaborative and inclusive team environment. This is particularly important when using a democratic or laissez-faire leadership style.

Monitor and evaluate effectiveness

Regularly assess how well the styles you're adopting are working and be open to making changes if necessary. Solicit feedback from team members and colleagues to get a sense of how well you are matching style to situation.

Practice flexibility

The most effective leaders are those who can adapt their style to fit the needs of their team, and the specific tasks on which they are working. Be open to trying different styles and be willing to adapt as needed.

Thought starters

- Which of Lewin's styles do you typically use, and is this always the most effective?
- Consider other leaders in your organisation and the styles they use. Which are most effective for them, and why?
- How does leadership style affect your experience as a team member? What are the benefits and difficulties with the leadership styles you have experienced?
- How might you use different leadership styles in different situations? When might an authoritarian style be most effective, and when might a democratic or laissez-faire style be more appropriate?
- How might you incorporate some of the key ideas from Lewin's leadership styles framework into your own leadership practice?

What next?

Read *The Nine Types of Leader: How the Leaders of Tomorrow Can Learn from the Leaders of Today* by James Ashton.

34

Situational leadership

Adapting your leadership style to context and priorities

The big picture

Situational leadership theory was developed by Paul Hersey and Ken Blanchard in the 1960s and 70s. Widely used in management and leadership training ever since, it is based on the belief that a "one size fits all" approach to leadership is inadequate; instead, leaders and managers need to adapt their approach to the specific needs and abilities of the individuals or team being led. The theory is based on the levels of willingness and experience (commitment and competence) of team members, and the leadership required to maximise people's development and achieve desired outcomes.

Situational leadership became a vital part of the approach that highlighted the need for rigour, detail, specificity and real-world relevance in leadership and management. The theory became part of the behaviouralist approach to leadership, which places a focus on behaviours rather than innate personal traits and characteristics – for example, that leaders were born, not made; that leaders were invariably male and had other stereotypical qualities such as being commanding, decisive and certain.

Hersey and Blanchard's thoughtful, practical model provides constructive criticism of this approach and encourages leaders and organisations to understand what different styles of leadership are needed, and how and when to deploy them.

About the idea

Hersey and Blanchard's insight was to recognise that different people have different levels of competence and commitment, and that effective leadership – getting the best out of people – involves adjusting leadership styles to match the abilities of the people involved and the situation or task at hand.

They identified four main leadership styles:

- directing
- coaching
- supporting
- delegating.

Understanding these four leadership styles helps leaders to choose the appropriate style, not just to ensure that the work is completed effectively, but also to help people progress to the next level of competence.

The categories of situation and leadership style are as follows.

Low competence, high commitment

This category includes people who lack the skills and experience needed to complete a task or achieve a goal but are motivated and enthusiastic. For these people, the appropriate leadership style is *directing*, where the leader provides clear instructions and closely supervises their work.

Some competence, low commitment

This category includes people who have some knowledge and skills but lack the confidence or motivation to work independently. In this situation, the appropriate leadership style is *coaching*, where the leader provides guidance and support to build confidence and commitment.

Moderate to high competence, variable commitment

This category includes people who have the knowledge and skills to complete a task or achieve a goal but may lack confidence or motivation in certain areas. For people in this category the appropriate leadership style is *supporting*, where the leader provides feedback and support to reinforce positive behaviours, helps the individual overcome any obstacles, and builds confidence and commitment.

High competence, high commitment

This category includes people who have the knowledge, skills and motivation to complete a task or achieve a goal with little or no guidance or support. For these individuals the appropriate style is *delegating*, where the leader provides an individual with the autonomy to progress or complete the task independently.

Crucially, the context and the task at hand are hugely significant too. For example, a surgeon highlighted the fact that she could, with relative ease, conduct two operations simultaneously. This is because part of the skill of a surgeon lies in the ability to know when to direct and take charge, when to delegate (for example, closing the wound can be done by a more junior colleague), and when, as well as how, to provide coaching and support for colleagues who are learning.

Situational leadership has been criticised for being too simplistic: four categories may be an improvement on past conceptions of leadership, but they do not take sufficient account of the nuances and complexities of leadership in practice. It is also argued that it places too much emphasis on the leader's style and neglects the needs and preferences of followers. Today, leadership is seen as much more of a two-way relationship and is much more attuned to different cultural contexts.

However, the idea that management and leadership need to take into account the people involved and the situation remains a practical and useful (if somewhat rudimentary) way to approach the task of managing and leading a range of people with varying levels of skills and motivation.

In practice

What is the best way to lead? The answer is that it depends – on the context, the level of urgency, jeopardy or risk, the people around you, past experience, the level of skill needed, and much else besides. When it comes to leadership, one size definitely does not fit every situation. With this in mind, several simple steps can help.

Be open and seek to understand

This openness starts with you: what does the situation feel like, and how easy is it for you to progress or resolve? When it comes to leading others, situational leadership starts with the ability to assess someone's competence and commitment. This means focusing on a person's knowledge, skills and attitude (including their confidence levels) to the task or goal at hand, usually through observation, feedback and discussion.

Adapt your style

Based on that understanding, you can then adopt the most appropriate styles or approaches. This will change over time. When someone becomes more experienced or is more engaged, or if you're working on a different task, then your style needs to shift too.

Provide communication, feedback and support

Situational leadership highlights the need to provide continuing feedback and support to help people to develop and learn. This can include coaching, mentoring and training, as well as recognition and rewards for performance.

Monitor progress

Situational leadership emphasises the importance of regularly assessing development needs, which should evolve over time, as part of continuing diagnosis.

Thought starters

- How do you effectively assess someone's competence and commitment when working with them? How could you improve your assessment?
- How effective is your communication with colleagues? How do you communicate in the right way, at the right time?
- How do you provide the most effective leadership style (directing, coaching, supporting and delegating) at the right time? How could this improve?
- What is your approach to leading and working with others – for example, in a project team? Is it sufficiently flexible and adaptable?
- What are the potential challenges of implementing a situational leadership approach?

What next?

Review the resources and insights available from the Center for Leadership Studies: www.situational.com

35

Charan's leadership pipeline

Identifying, developing and supporting leaders at all levels

The big picture

The leadership pipeline model was developed by Ram Charan, Stephen Drotter and James Noel in their 2001 book *The Leadership Pipeline: How to Build the Leadership Powered Company*. It offers a framework for identifying, developing and supporting leaders, and is based on work done at General Electric in the 1970s by business analyst Walter Mahler. The model is widely regarded as an important and relevant contribution to thinking about leaders and leadership development.

Charan et al. argue that traditional approaches to leadership development have focused on strengthening existing skills rather than learning new skills. The leadership pipeline recognises that improvements in an individual's performance is most effective when new skills are built on a solid foundation of existing skills acquired at previous levels of leadership, and when people are given the time and support to learn the skills required for their next role.

The pipeline framework looks at what needs to be in place to create a pipeline of leaders for the present and preparing for the future. It defines six critical leadership pathways to assess competence, leader development and capability growth to address challenges at each stage of the pipeline.

About the idea

The leadership pipeline model follows six significant events in any leader's career. They represent transitions that cannot be mastered in a day or by a course; they are skills which need to be mastered through practice and supported by leaders and peers. The purpose of the framework is to enable leaders and organisations to succeed today, while preparing for the future – with the expertise embedded in the organisation. The successful development of a robust leadership pipeline requires new behaviours, attitudes and skills from the most senior leadership levels, and mirrored down the line.

The model defines six critical levels, and is based on the belief that career progression involves making successful transitions at each level:

1. from managing yourself to managing others
2. from managing others to managing managers
3. from managing managers to functional director
4. from functional director to business director
5. from business director to group business director
6. from group business director to enterprise manager.

Charan et al. argue that people often make these career transitions without the relevant support or preparation. Instead, they tend to mirror the behaviour of their predecessors and develop a way of working through trial and error. The leadership pipeline defines the skills and attributes required for success at each level across three key areas:

- values
- time management
- new skills.

People need to acquire all the skills and behaviours at each level before moving to the next. This consistent focus on skills, time management and values improves performance and benefits both individuals and organisations.

Contemporary perspectives recognise that the qualities and actions associated with leadership can be shown by people at different levels within and across an organisation who often bring invaluable credibility, experience and expertise. This viewpoint – encapsulated by the term *distributed* leadership – challenges the traditional notion that leadership is solely associated with formal positions or titles. It emphasises the importance of collaboration, empowerment and collective decision-making.

Although the leadership pipeline model is based on a more traditional hierarchical approach to leadership development, it is not necessarily incompatible with this idea. It remains an important tool for recognising and developing leadership potential at all levels, providing opportunities for skill development, encouraging collaboration and shared decision-making, and fostering a culture that values and supports people, wherever they may be on an organisational chart.

In practice

Charan's leadership pipeline emphasises the importance of identifying, developing and supporting managers and leaders through the six key passages, building capability at all levels and over time. It highlights the need for people to develop their skills and mindset as they progress through different leadership levels, aligning their capabilities with the increasing complexity and strategic demands of their roles.

At each stage, people need to be clear about the capabilities needed to operate consistently, transparently and effectively. They also need to develop and master the skills needed for the future. Mastering the transitions between levels can be difficult; understanding what those transitions mean is the first step to that mastery.

Passage 1. From managing yourself to managing others

This is often the most challenging transition. It involves a shift from delivering results to delivering through others. It means understanding and thinking about the needs of others and the business as a whole. Many first-time managers try to continue doing their old job while attempting to master their new one; instead, they need to stop and learn how to balance the two. For example, if you are managing a newly formed team, you will need to have an eye on team dynamics and how tasks are allocated as well as making time for the tasks that you yourself need to complete, which will require you to teach, coach and delegate.

Passage 2. From managing others to managing managers

The manager of managers' priorities typically includes driving productivity and delivering results through others, while having less direct hands-on involvement; communication and leadership passes through other direct reports. This is a vital stage: a poor manager of managers can have a large impact on an organisation's performance and productivity.

Passage 3. From managing managers to functional director

The transition into functional management (for example, leading a sales or production or a larger project team) requires a manager to take on work in areas that are unfamiliar, and where they will have to rely on the expertise of others. The manager should work collaboratively, sharing their understanding and learnings along the way, growing their expertise and bringing others along with them too.

Passage 4. From functional director to business director

This transition leads to a greater level of autonomy, with the business manager working with greater levels of responsibility and balancing multiple functions or teams. It is at this level that a manager becomes more involved in setting and implementing organisation-wide strategic plans.

Succeeding with this transition is best achieved by spending time "on the ground" with functional managers in the business – understanding their needs and challenges and setting goals to keep track of the business and the emergence of potential problems.

Passage 5. From business director to group business director

This transition is from managing a single business to managing a portfolio of businesses, ensuring that each one is successful as well as the whole portfolio. Managers at this stage are deeply involved in setting business and group strategy and targets. This requires new skills, insights and different styles: leading others, managing finance, executing strategy, leading communication and interacting with customers.

Passage 6. From group business director to enterprise manager

This final transition requires a different set of skills to other levels and is the culmination of the previous transitions. An enterprise manager is an individual who is a senior member of an organisation responsible for wide-ranging aspects of operations on a broader scale, typically managing multiple departments and budget lines. This person must lead with clear values and beliefs, facing many more pressures from a wider range of stakeholders. An effective enterprise manager is adept at balancing external stakeholder needs with short- and long-term business needs, as well as setting a clear long-term strategy while managing and motivating a team of senior level leaders with their own complex needs.

In practice, the nature of the six transitions in the leadership pipeline framework vary depending on the organisation, the people involved, the sector and the organisation's culture and context. Customised to suit organisational needs, the pipeline model can help people develop the skills they need to match the job they need to do and the level at which they are operating.

Using the leadership pipeline framework

For people looking to apply the leadership pipeline, two questions are especially relevant. What do I need to do to succeed in my current role? And what should I do now to prepare for my next role? These questions apply wherever you are in the pipeline.

For senior leaders and others responsible for developing and promoting their colleagues, the questions are more nuanced and context-specific. Typical questions might include: are the requirements for all our roles up to date and relevant? Are we finding and developing people with potential? In fact, are we doing enough to support and develop people at all levels, so they can progress through the pipeline?

Thought starters

- What are the implications of the leadership pipeline for your career? Are you actively mastering your current role and preparing for the next one?
- Can you map your organisation's structure to the leadership pipeline framework?
- How well does the current people development process in your organisation prepare individuals to take on new roles and responsibilities?
- How can your organisation use the leadership pipeline model to create a strong leadership succession plan?
- How can the leadership pipeline model be integrated with other leadership development approaches or models?

What next?

Read *The Leadership Pipeline* by Ram Charan, Stephen Drotter and James Noel.

36

Belbin team roles

Understanding and improving how teams work

The big picture

The work of British psychologist Meredith Belbin has shone a lasting light on one of the most common yet challenging aspects of work: understanding and improving the way that teams operate. Belbin identified nine different types of behaviour, or roles, that are needed in a successful team. Understanding these roles can be invaluable when building, leading or simply working in a team.

A significant part of Belbin's research looked at how teams work in practice. By exploring group and individual behaviour within a broad range of teams, Belbin developed his theory of *team roles*, with the central insight that each individual working in a team has a preferred role and an approach that they favour. People may exhibit the characteristics of several roles, but one or two styles tend to dominate. Crucially, team roles are about behaviours, not personality traits. This means that people can assume different roles and be developed to adopt a team role: their initial preference is not fixed or permanent.

Until the 1980s employees were broadly divided into workers and managers (or leaders). Belbin's work highlighted the dynamics of the unit between individuals and the organisation: the team. Although thinking about team dynamics and teamworking has evolved significantly since the 1980s, Belbin's work still provides a benchmark and starting point for a rigorous and methodical understanding, and analysis, of team dynamics.

About the idea

Understanding the roles that people play in a team is valuable for each member of the team. It is also helpful for the manager of the team, and above all it provides a useful tool for the team to manage and develop its own effectiveness.

Belbin's nine team roles can be grouped into three broad categories: action, thinking and social. No role is more valuable than any other and each role has its strengths – the contribution it brings – and what Belbin calls "allowable weaknesses". What matters is the balance of roles and role categories within a team. The nine roles do not mean that teams need at least nine people displaying the nine behaviours. But Belbin suggests that having access to a range of behaviours across his three categories can make even the smallest teams more successful.

The nine Belbin roles are shown in Table 7.

Although Belbin suggests that individuals tend to adopt a particular team role, behaviour within a team can vary according to the context, the goals being pursued, team relationships and the team leader, as well as the culture and experience of team members, and the overall situation.

Understanding the Belbin team roles model can stimulate discussion, focusing team members on their strengths, weaknesses, the role they can play and the explicit contributions they can make to the successful and harmonious working of the team. The model also provides a unifying language and shared understanding for identifying and improving team dynamics.

In practice

Belbin's team roles model is a valuable tool for anyone wanting to identify contributions as well as potential strengths and weaknesses within a team. Crucially, as team roles concern behaviours and not personality traits, people can adopt different team roles if required by a particular set of circumstances, or simply to increase the team's balance and overall effectiveness.

Belbin team roles

TABLE 7: THE NINE BELBIN ROLES, WITH THEIR STRENGTHS AND WEAKNESSES

Action-oriented roles	Strengths	Allowable weaknesses
1. Implementer	Disciplined, reliable and efficient Turns ideas into practical actions and results	Can be inflexible or slow to respond to new possibilities
2. Completer finisher	Conscientious, anxious and seeks out errors and omissions Delivers on time	Can worry unduly (unsettling) and be reluctant to delegate
3. Shaper	Challenging and dynamic; thrives on the pressure of decision-making and problem-solving Has the drive and courage to overcome obstacles	Prone to provocation May offend people's feelings

Thinking-oriented roles	Strengths	Allowable weaknesses
4. Plant	Creative, imaginative, unorthodox Solves difficult problems	Ignores details Can be too preoccupied to communicate well
5. Specialist	Single-minded, self-starting and dedicated Provides valuable knowledge and skills that may be in short supply	Concentrates on technicalities May contribute on only a narrow front
6. Monitor evaluator	Sober, strategic and discerning Views all options and has sound, accurate judgement	Lacks drive and the ability to inspire others

Socially oriented roles	Strengths	Allowable weaknesses
7. Resource investigator	Extrovert, enthusiastic, communicative Explores opportunities and develops contacts – vital when researching and implementing decisions	Over-optimistic Can lose interest once initial enthusiasm has passed
8. Coordinator	Mature, confident and a good organiser Clarifies goals, promotes decisions and delegates well	Can be seen as manipulative and sometimes offloads work
9. Teamworker	Cooperative, perceptive and diplomatic Listens, builds and averts friction	Can be indecisive in crunch situations

Understand people's strengths and preferred roles

Identifying each team member's typical team role or preference can foster greater understanding within the team of each person's contribution. These may match, overlap or contrast with those of their colleagues; discussing these issues generates greater understanding, appreciation and connection within the team, as well as potentially leading to more effective teamworking and mutual support.

Reflect on the whole team

Think about the team. Are any roles missing, or is there excessive duplication between team types and roles? For example, if your team is looking to diversify, you'll almost certainly want to see some plant-type behaviours to generate new ideas. But you'll also – at the very least – need some shaper behaviours to help refine those ideas, an implementer to plan for execution and a teamworker to make sure everyone is involved and on board with the ideas being discussed.

Discuss how to achieve the best balance of roles

It can be useful to ask team members for three actions based on their understanding of mutual strengths and allowable weaknesses: what opportunities does this team configuration provide? What are the priorities, and where are the areas of vulnerability? How will these be addressed?

Thought starters

- What role do you typically play in teams?
- What additional team roles could you develop and adopt?
- What are your strengths and weaknesses as a team member?
- When do you do your best work in teams? When do you typically struggle?

- Does your team have a clear charter or set of rules for the way you work? Are there agreed ways of behaving and interacting, a clear purpose, a way of measuring progress or success, and an agreed (and regularly updated) set of priorities?

What next?

Take a look at the resources on the Belbin website: www.Belbin.com

37

Tuckman's stages of team development

How team dynamics evolve and change

The big picture

What's it like to be part of your team at work? Are you a high-performing unit, working as a well-oiled machine towards clear goals, supporting each other and having fun along the way? Or are there times where your team can seem less than the sum of its parts, leading to frustration and even conflict?

Even the best teams have times when things go less well, which is why an understanding of how teams typically operate – their dynamics – can help to smooth the path to team success. Tuckman's stages of team development is a model at the heart of this thinking.

Bruce Tuckman was an American psychologist who studied group dynamics and the ways in which teams form, develop and function. He first proposed the four stages of his team development model – forming, storming, norming and performing – in 1965.

The model is based on the idea that teams typically go through a series of stages as they form and mature. These stages describe the different challenges and dynamics that teams encounter as they work together, evolve and change.

Tuckman's stages of team development have been widely adopted and are used in a variety of settings, including business, education and sports. They are seen as a useful way to understand and improve team performance.

About the idea

The ultimate goal for any team is to work efficiently, effectively and in harmony and Tuckman proposed that there are four stages through which teams pass before they reach this goal.

Forming is when the team is coming together and is focused on establishing structure and getting to know each other. Members may be uncertain about their roles and responsibilities and may be cautious in their interactions with one another.

Storming is a challenging stage, with conflict and disagreement potentially arising as team members start to express their opinions and ideas. This can lead to tension and conflict within the team as members work to establish their roles and relationships.

Norming occurs when the team starts to work through its conflicts and establish clear roles and responsibilities. Team members begin to work together more cohesively and effectively, with trust, collaboration and mutual support starting to build.

Performing is the final stage, with the team working together effectively and efficiently to achieve its goals. Team members have a strong sense of teamwork and can address conflicts and challenges in a constructive way.

In an update to his model, Bruce Tuckman and Mary Ann Jensen introduced a fifth stage – *adjourning* – that refers to the process of the team disbanding or transitioning after completing its project or achieving its goals. This stage involves wrapping up loose ends, celebrating achievements and acknowledging the ending of the team's journey. It recognises that teams sometimes have a life cycle, and that closure is an important part of the team's development process.

Although these four (or five) stages are sequential, progress is not always linear. Teams can get "stuck" at certain stages – especially storming – or can move up and down the stages as team dynamics change (for example, if someone joins, leaves or is promoted). The model allows team members to recognise when this is happening, adapt and move forward. It offers a simple framework to recognise a team's current state and guide members to resolutions.

It has been argued that Tuckman's model does not pay sufficient attention to team context or culture: the circumstances in which a team operates may be an important factor in how the team develops, functions and performs. But used alongside other ideas about teams (see chapters 36 and 38), it is a useful tool for understanding and monitoring team dynamics and their impact on behaviours and performance.

In practice

Tuckman's stages of team development describe the natural progression of teams from forming (getting acquainted), to storming (potential for conflict), to norming (cohesion and collaboration), to performing (high performance). The model highlights the importance of recognising and addressing conflicts, while establishing trust and cooperation to help teams reach their full potential.

Here's how you can use it.

Assess your team's stage of development

Are you still forming? Stuck in storming? High performing? Thinking this through can help you understand the specific challenges and dynamics your team might be facing and tailor your approach to the team's needs.

Set the vision

Teams need a clear vision and shared objectives to guide their work; without these, the team can fragment because of confusion. Once you have identified the stage that your team is in, the next step is to revisit that vision and shared objectives to make sure they are clear and drive how you will work together to achieve your aims. This will help the team focus on specific areas for improvement and track its progress.

Engage in team-building activities

Tuckman's model is a useful framework for planning team-building activities, so that teams progress through the different stages and become more effective. For example, activities that focus on establishing clear roles and responsibilities may be particularly useful during the forming and storming stages. Co-creating a team charter, to establish and agree roles, responsibilities, expectations and reporting may help at this stage. Once you move towards the norming and performing stages, you might switch to activities that focus on how you will communicate and collaborate.

Provide training and development

Tuckman's stages of team development can be used as a framework for designing training programmes that help teams develop the skills and competencies they need to progress both individually and as a member of the team.

Coach and support team members

Support people as they progress through the different stages of team development. This includes providing feedback and coaching, facilitating open communication and collaboration, and helping team members resolve conflicts and challenges.

Bear in mind that the specific needs and characteristics of the team, as well as other factors such as team culture and context, will also contribute to team effectiveness. Tuckman's model also assumes that the conditions are right for the team to thrive, such as clear vision, the right resources, and the time and space to deliver (see Chapter 38 on enabling conditions). The chances are that, by applying the model to diagnose a team's performance, these wider issues will also become clear.

Thought starters

- Identify the current stage of your team's development and outline the specific challenges and dynamics associated with it.

- How can you use Tuckman's stages of team development as a framework for setting goals and objectives for your team?
- What team-building activities or training programmes might be most useful for your team in its current stage?
- How can you support team members as they progress through the different stages of team development?
- How can you use Tuckman's stages of team development to identify areas for improvement and track your team's progress over time?

What next?

Read *Building Top-Performing Teams* by Lucy Widdowson and Paul J. Barbour.

38

Hackman's enabling conditions for teams

The factors teams need to achieve high performance

The big picture

Bruce Tuckman's stages of team development model looks to a team's *internal* dynamics. Other thinking about teams suggests that this is only half of the story: teams also need to operate in a climate that gives its members the best chance of success.

In his 2002 book *Leading Teams,* organisational psychologist Richard Hackman identified six enabling conditions that are necessary for any team to be successful. Hackman had observed that organisations tend to be either too directive with teams, telling them what to do and how to do it, or too vague, with teams left to set their own objectives and organise ways of working together that result in inefficiencies.

Focusing on the six enabling conditions gives teams the best possible chance of achieving their goals and making the most of their potential.

About the idea

Hackman's thinking was based on the idea that, to create the right conditions for a team to be successful, a team leader needs to:

- understand the key enabling conditions and be able to strengthen them over time
- know how to get things done such as articulating clear goals

- demonstrate good emotional intelligence (see Chapter 2) to know when to be more directive and when to be less directive, in response to the needs of the team.

The six enabling conditions are as follows.

1. *Clear goals.* Teams need to have clear and specific goals that are understood by all members. This helps everyone stay focused and motivated by outcomes.

2. *Interdependence.* Team members should have a high level of interdependence, meaning that their work is interconnected and collaborative, and they rely on each other to get things done.

3. *A supportive organisational context.* The team should have the resources, support and autonomy it needs to be successful.

4. *Norms of mutual support.* Team members should have mutual respect and provide support for each other.

5. *Role clarity.* Team members need a clear understanding of their roles and responsibilities within the team, and these should not duplicate. The team also needs to know who is in the team and what role each person plays.

6. *An effective team structure.* The team should have a structure that allows it to work efficiently and effectively. This might include things like clear lines of communication and decision-making processes.

By establishing and maintaining these enabling conditions a team is ideally positioned to achieve its goals and be successful. The conditions create an environment that allows the team to work efficiently and effectively towards its shared goals.

Alongside these enabling conditions there are several other factors which contribute to a team's success and should also be considered, as Hackman acknowledged.

Team members' skills and abilities. A team with a diverse set of skills and abilities is better equipped to handle a wide range of tasks and challenges.

External factors. A team's environment and resources can also affect its performance. A team with access to the necessary tools, equipment and support is more likely to succeed than a team without the resources they need to achieve their goals.

Leadership. The way a leader manages their team also plays a significant role in the team's success. A leader who is supportive, empowering and transparent can create a positive team culture that promotes success.

Today, you would add other factors such as the power of diversity of thought, or external factors that might compromise the conditions such as competing priorities that could undermine interdependence.

In practice

The essence of Hackman's ideas is that effective team leadership involves creating conditions for the team to thrive, such as providing a clear and meaningful purpose, fostering a supportive and collaborative environment, and establishing appropriate team composition and structure.

Successful team leaders should focus on the team's performance and development over time rather than just immediate outcomes. Leaders should understand the unique dynamics and challenges of each team they lead.

In practice, to create the right enabling conditions, team leaders need to do the following.

Set clear goals

Define specific, measurable, achievable, relevant and time-bound (SMART) objectives for the team (see Chapter 39). This helps team members understand their direction and how their work fits into the bigger picture.

Foster interdependence

Assign tasks that require team members to work together and rely on each other to get things done. Encourage open communication and sharing of resources to promote collaboration.

Provide support and resources

Make sure the team has the resources and support it needs to be successful, including access to training, equipment and information. This includes giving people enough time to complete their work.

Promote norms of mutual support

Make clear expectations on behaviours for team members, whether they are working together or with others. Encourage team members to support and respect each other and model this behaviour yourself.

Clarify roles and responsibilities

Clearly define each team member's roles and responsibilities, and regularly review and update these roles as needed.

Establish an effective team structure

Set up clear lines of communication, decision-making processes and protocols for handling conflicts to create an effective team structure.

Thought starters

- How could a focus on Hackman's enabling conditions improve your team performance?
- What are your team's goals and objectives? Are they clear and specific?
- Are team roles and responsibilities clear? Does everyone know who is doing what?
- How can tasks be structured to foster interdependence among team members?

- How can norms of mutual support be promoted within the team?

What next?

Read *Leading Teams: Setting the Stage for Great Performances* by J. Richard Hackman.

39

SMART goal setting

Fuelling success with realistic and achievable goals

The big picture

Goal setting has developed as a powerful, effective and popular way to help people and organisations focus on achieving agreed priorities. The process of setting goals involves defining clear objectives, creating a roadmap for achieving them, and measuring progress.

As a process, it needs to take a dynamic approach that goes beyond mere wishful thinking. It involves practice, careful planning, execution, adaptation and communication.

One of the earliest advocates of goal setting was Edwin Locke, whose 1968 article "Toward a theory of task motivation and incentives" highlighted the fact that people are motivated by well-defined goals and constructive feedback, and consequently more likely to accomplish these goals when they are specific and measurable.

Since then, a range of goal-setting techniques and models has been developed, including the idea of SMART goals (sometimes accredited to Locke himself), an acronym that reinforces the idea that setting specific goals with the right level of challenge, supported by feedback and commitment, can be a powerful tool for personal and professional success. It's a technique encapsulated by the words of the management thinker Peter Drucker, who highlighted the truth that "what gets measured, gets managed".

About the idea

SMART is an acronym that represents the criteria for setting goals effectively.

Specific

By being clear and specific, there is no room for ambiguity. A specific goal answers the questions: What do I want to accomplish? Why is it important? How will I achieve it?

Measurable

Measurable goals make it easier to track progress and determine when the goal(s) are successfully met. To do this, any goal must have quantifiable and tangible criteria associated with it from the outset.

Achievable

The right level of challenge is good, but the best goals are also realistic and achievable and take into account available resources and time. Unachievable goals are demotivating.

Relevant

Goals must align with overall objectives at a team and organisational level (or, if personal, with your own values and long-term objectives). They need to make sense in the broader context of your life or work.

Time-bound

There must be a defined timeframe or deadline. This adds a sense of urgency and momentum, helping with effective time management and prioritisation.

So, rather than just asking someone to "boost social media engagement", a SMART goal would specify the need to "secure 15% more Instagram followers in Q1".

Here are some other well-known frameworks commonly used or adapted.

Objectives and key results (OKRs). Objectives: define what needs to be achieved. Key results: establish specific, measurable outcomes to indicate progress.

Key performance indicators (KPIs). Identify and set goals based on key metrics that indicate success in various areas of performance.

Personal development plans (PDPs). A summary of personal goals, outlining opportunities for growth and personal and professional development.

Backward goal setting. Define the ultimate goal and then work backwards to identify the steps needed to reach that goal.

Management by objectives (MBO). Setting goals collaboratively between managers and employees to focus on alignment and buy-in.

Big, hairy, audacious goals (BHAGs). Ambitious, long-term goals designed to push an organisation beyond its normal limits to become a unifying focal point.

The methodology or approach you use will depend on your context: whether you are setting personal or business goals, and the nature of the goals being set.

Combining elements from different methods may also be effective in creating a comprehensive goal-setting strategy.

In practice

The SMART framework is just one example of a model or process for goal setting and, like all similar goal-setting models, it involves articulating what you want to achieve (the goal) and clarifying how you will work to achieve it.

There are two main types of goal.

1. *End goals or objectives.* For example, "We will sell 1,000 units of our new product in the first year" is an end goal.

2. *Performance goals with continuous aims.* For example, "We will develop a coaching culture where people routinely receive feedback and support" is a performance goal.

Whatever methodology you choose, a goal-setting process typically includes the following elements.

Define the objectives – and prioritise

First, define the objectives. You need to articulate clearly what you want to achieve. This could be personal or professional, short term or long term. Also important is prioritisation. You need to identify the most important goals on which to focus your time and energy.

Develop motivation

When goals are well defined and relevant, you are more likely to stay committed to them. Good goals can be a source of inspiration, providing purpose and direction and enabling you to work towards something meaningful.

Goals are important criteria for decision-making. They will help you evaluate whether an action aligns with your desired outcome.

Monitor and measure progress

Establishing measurable indicators enables you to track progress and give quantifiable data for review and modification, as needed.

Feedback is also important. Checking progress regularly makes it possible to make necessary modifications. When circumstances change, goals should be adjusted to remain relevant and aligned with evolving priorities.

Make the most of your goals

Goals will help you identify key tasks and activities, reducing the likelihood of distraction and/or of being overwhelmed. Setting deadlines and timeframes enhances efficiency and prevents procrastination. It also encourages continuous learning and development by pushing people to acquire new skills and knowledge.

In organisational settings, goal setting aligns teams towards common objectives, fostering collaboration and synergy. Goals also provide a focus for communication. Clearly communicated goals ensure that everyone understands the collective vision and their role in achieving it.

Use goals as a framework for overcoming obstacles and setbacks, encouraging people to persevere in the face of difficulties and challenges.

Celebrate achievements

Don't forget to celebrate when goals have been achieved. Achieving goals gives a sense of accomplishment, and recognising these successes reinforces motivation and commitment.

Thought starters

- What are the priority outcomes that you want to achieve?
- How can you use SMART goals for your career or personal life?
- What is the best goal-setting approach for you?
- Are you working to realistic and reasonable timeframes?
- Are you getting (or giving) feedback to help achieve your goals?

What next?

Read *Goals! How To Get Everything You Want – Faster Than You Ever Thought Possible* by Brian Tracy.

40

Maslow's hierarchy of needs

Understanding motivation

The big picture

Millions of words have been spoken and committed to paper in search of that most elusive of workplace skills: how to motivate people to do what you need them to do. It's a field of research that has a long history beyond the world of work, with thinkers from a range of disciplines exploring why humans do the things they do and behave in the ways they behave. It's clear from the research that when people are motivated to do their jobs or go that extra mile, that makes a material difference both to their own experience at work and to performance and productivity. So how is that achieved? Let's go back in time to explore.

The hierarchy of needs, first introduced by American psychologist Abraham Maslow in 1943, is based on the idea that meeting people's needs is the key to motivating them. For Maslow, people have a hierarchy of needs, starting with their basic physiological needs and building with increasing complexity to include safety and security, love and belonging, self-esteem, and finally self-actualisation, with people able to achieve their full potential and find fulfilment. Visually, the theory is often shown as a pyramid, with self-actualisation as the pinnacle.

At work, Maslow's hierarchy shows that, when people's needs are met, they are more likely to feel motivated and engaged in their work, leading to increased productivity and job satisfaction. His focus on needs has contributed to the creation of work environments that are safe, engaging and supportive in the service of motivating them better.

Maslow's central idea took an early psychology-based approach to understanding motivation. It put thought and rigour into the previously neglected issue of motivation. Although by today's standards it may seem rudimentary and unsophisticated, it remains the foundation for a range of needs-based theories about how to get the best out of people at work.

About the idea

Maslow identified five types of need which must be met in order of lowest to highest. People are motivated to move up the hierarchy to fulfil their needs after these have been satisfied at each level. Once lower-level needs are met, they become less important, and higher-level needs become the focus of motivation. Ultimately, Maslow's hierarchy of needs suggests that individuals seek to reach a state of self-actualisation.

The five levels of the hierarchy are listed here, from the bottom upwards.

Physiological needs

These are the most basic and include food, water, shelter and other biological necessities. These needs must be met for an individual to survive.

In a work context, people need to access these basic needs through factors such as fair wages, a comfortable working environment, and adequate breaks for meals and rest.

Safety needs

Once physiological needs are met, individuals seek to fulfil their need for safety and security. This includes protection from harm and a safe environment.

At work, these needs are fulfilled by job security and a regard for people's health and safety at work, both of which can help to reduce anxiety and stress, leading to higher productivity.

Love and belonging needs

Once physiological and safety needs are met, individuals seek social connections and a sense of belonging. This includes relationships with family and friends, and a sense of community.

People who feel a sense of belonging and connection at work are more likely to be motivated. This is achieved through positive relationships with colleagues and a sense of community within the workplace.

Esteem needs

After the lower-level needs are met, individuals seek recognition, respect and a sense of achievement. This includes feeling valued and respected by others and having a sense of self-worth.

These needs are fulfilled at work by opportunities for career advancement, recognition for effort and achievement, and a sense of accomplishment through challenging and rewarding work.

Self-actualisation needs

The highest level of the hierarchy involves fulfilling one's potential and achieving personal growth. This includes pursuing creative or intellectual interests, developing personal values and achieving a sense of purpose.

At work, this means providing opportunities for continuing education and professional development, as well as creating the space for employees to pursue their interests and passions.

Maslow's thinking was developed in the 1950s and 60s by fellow psychologist Frederick Herzberg.

Herzberg's two-factor theory is based on the idea that the needs-based factors underpinning motivation fall into two distinct categories: *hygiene* and *motivation* factors.

Hygiene factors include adequate remuneration, job security, good working conditions and positive interpersonal relationships. If these needs are met, people will not be *dissatisfied* at work. However, on their own, these factors will not necessarily lead to increased motivation.

This is where Herzberg's motivation factors come in. Once people's hygiene factor needs are met, they will look to meet motivation factor needs, such as the right level of challenge and support, job responsibility, and opportunities for growth and development. These motivation factors increase *satisfaction* – and therefore motivation – at work.

The writer Daniel Pink took up these themes in his 2009 book *Drive: The Surprising Truth About What Motivates Us.*

Pink reminds us that another way to think about motivation is in terms of *extrinsic* (external) and *intrinsic* (internal) motivation.

- Extrinsic motivation is based on a classic carrot and stick approach, focused on rewards or avoiding sanctions.
- Intrinsic motivation is about meeting people's internal need for personal growth and development.

For Pink, extrinsic motivators can take you only so far. They might work in the short term and when tasks are simple and measurement of results is straightforward. They are much less likely to motivate people who are doing work that requires cognitive skill and sophisticated thinking and where the results are longer term and less obvious.

For these kinds of knowledge workers, it's all about those intrinsic motivators, summarised in Pink's three motivation factors.

1. *Autonomy*: feeling empowered and in control of your work.
2. *Mastery:* the feeling of fulfilment that comes from being skilled and doing a job well, or completing a difficult task.
3. *Purpose*: the desire to do meaningful work that has value and contributes to a wider purpose.

If these three factors are present at work, people are much more likely to be motivated.

In practice

Motivation is personal: what motivates you will not necessarily motivate your colleagues. Everyone is unique and has specific needs that drive their own motivations. But keeping in mind Maslow's fundamental idea that people's needs must be met for them to be motivated in their work will help you to identify and make the most of the range of factors that can motivate you as well as others.

For example, someone who appears isolated and struggles to contribute may be at Maslow's love and belonging stage, and so would benefit from greater inclusion, camaraderie and praise. If a colleague is struggling to pay the rent, Herzberg's motivator factors are unlikely to hit the mark and hygiene factors might need to be addressed. If you have keen and capable people in your team, make sure they have the autonomy and mastery they need to get on with the job – and that they understand how what they do contributes to team and organisational purpose.

The following steps will also help.

Understand the limits of remuneration as a motivator. Even the juiciest carrot might not meet long-term, intrinsic motivation needs.

Consider whether hygiene factors are affecting motivation. If they are, identify what they are and what can be done to address them.

Think about and discuss what would increase motivation, for yourself and others. Are there opportunities for career development and progression, for example? Would a bit of healthy competition work for some people?

Develop autonomy. Are you and your colleagues masters of your own work, receiving the right balance of guidance and support and independence?

Work on your mastery and enable others too. Nothing beats that feeling of fulfilment and accomplishment when progress is made, obstacles overcome or success is achieved.

Find your purpose. This means finding within work a value and meaning that goes beyond personal benefit – and, ideally, connects with organisational purpose too.

Thought starters

- How motivated are you, and what would enhance or sustain your motivation?
- How motivated are your colleagues? What could you do to develop a more motivating work environment?
- Do you have the right level of autonomy in your work – the level that works best for you? If not, what can you do about it?
- Do you feel in control and expert in at least one part of your role? What is your purpose – the higher-order reason that you work beyond the basic needs?

What next?

Read *Drive: The Surprising Truth About What Motivates Us* by Daniel H. Pink.

41

Schein's three levels of organisational culture

Uncovering the assumptions that shape organisations

The big picture

American social psychologist Edgar Schein developed his model of organisational culture in the 1970s and 80s, introducing the concept in 1985 in his seminal book *Organisational Culture and Leadership*.

Schein's model provides a comprehensive framework for understanding the complex and multifaceted nature of organisational culture. It highlights the idea that culture is not just a superficial layer of visible artifacts, but rather a deep-seated set of underlying assumptions and values that shape the behaviour and attitudes of people at work.

The model also helps people gain a deeper understanding of the values, norms and beliefs that drive organisations by identifying and analysing different levels of culture. This insight can shape strategy, structure and processes in a way that aligns and works with, rather than against, culture.

About the idea

Schein's model of organisational culture identifies three levels that are important for understanding the underlying assumptions, beliefs and values that shape an organisation's behaviour and attitudes.

Artifacts

These are the visible and tangible elements of culture, such as the physical environment, dress codes, office layout, symbols and rituals. Artifacts are the most visible aspects of culture, and the easiest to observe, and they can provide clues about the deeper levels of culture too. For example, a dress code that emphasises formality and professionalism may reflect a culture that values traditionalism and adherence to established norms.

Espoused values

These are the stated values and norms of an organisation, such as mission statements, codes of conduct and performance objectives. Espoused values are the beliefs and attitudes that members of the organisation claim to hold and practice. These values are often communicated through official documents, speeches and other forms of communication. For example, an organisation that emphasises teamwork and collaboration may have values that emphasise cooperation, communication and mutual support.

Basic underlying assumptions

This level includes the unconscious, taken-for-granted beliefs and values that underlie the behaviour and attitudes of members of an organisation. Basic underlying assumptions are the deepest level of culture and are often difficult to identify and articulate. They are deeply ingrained in the culture of an organisation and may be communicated through non-verbal cues and social norms. For example, an organisation that values individualism and competition may have underlying assumptions that emphasise the importance of personal achievement and success.

Schein's model suggests that to truly understand an organisation's culture you need to explore all three levels. The framework can be used to diagnose the strengths and weaknesses of an organisation's culture, and to identify areas for improvement. For example, there could be a disconnect between espoused values with the underlying assumptions that drive behaviours that can create a lack of credibility. A company may say it values collaboration, but is this backed up by working practices and procedures and does it feel like that on the ground?

The model can also be used to help facilitate culture change by identifying the underlying assumptions that may be holding organisations back, and then working to shift those assumptions to align better with the desired outcome.

Culture is a tricky thing to measure, and Schein's thinking has been criticised for an overemphasis on the role of leaders, as opposed to other factors like group dynamics or external influences in shaping organisational culture and its limited emphasis on diversity and cultural difference.

Other thinkers have built on Schein's work to develop a range of ideas about how we understand organisational culture. The cultural web, for example, was developed by Gerry Johnson and Kevan Scholes in the 1990s. This breaks down the components of culture into more detailed, practical elements that can be more readily understood, managed and, over time, shaped.

For example, an organisation's culture is often clear from the control and rewards systems it has in place or the stories and myths that people tell about it.

An organisation with a deep history and clear purpose – like a professional body – is likely to have a more formal culture, manifested by strict hierarchies, rigorous control systems and formal meetings, committees and communications. At the other end of the cultural spectrum, a tech start-up is more likely to adopt cultural norms designed to support flexibility and agility, such as flatter structures, informal get-togethers and communication and light-touch control systems. Both these cultures are entirely appropriate for the different purposes and goals of the organisations. But a failure to understand the impact of the different cultural components at play might bring with it the risk that the more traditional organisations fail to evolve and the start-up might fail to scale effectively without the structures and systems needed to support growth.

Figure 7: **The culture web**

Source: From original diagram in *Fundamentals of Strategy* by Gerry Johnson, Richard Whittington and Kevan Scholes

In practice

The three levels of Schein's model – artifacts, espoused values and underlying assumptions – interact to create a deep-rooted and influential system that guides the behaviour and decision-making within, and across, an organisation.

Awareness of the three levels can be used to understand your organisation's culture and to support cultural change. Here are some practical points to consider.

Define your purpose

Identify the specific purpose or problem that you want to address using the model. For example, you may want to improve employee engagement, enhance innovation or align culture with strategy better.

Gather data on your culture

Use methods such as surveys, interviews, focus groups and observation. Use Schein's three levels of culture to guide the data-collection process.

Analyse the data

Identify the key artifacts, espoused values and underlying assumptions that shape the organisation's culture. Look for patterns and themes.

Identify strengths and weaknesses

Based on the analysis of the data, consider how the culture supports or hinders the organisation's goals and objectives. Is there alignment or a mismatch? Do espoused values feel real on the ground?

Develop recommendations for improvement

Looking at the strengths and weaknesses identified in the data analysis, consider how changes to the three elements might be used to create a more positive and effective culture in your organisation.

Implement changes and evaluate

Monitor the impact of the changes and adjust as needed. Evaluate the results of the culture change process to determine whether it has been effective in achieving the desired outcomes. Use feedback from employees, customers and other stakeholders to inform continuing improvements.

Thought starters

- How would you define the culture of your team or organisation, based either on Schein's model or the cultural web?
- In what way do your organisation's artifacts, espoused values and underlying assumptions differ or contradict each other?
- How could the culture in your team or organisation be improved? How could you make this happen?
- Are the culture and strategy of your organisation in line with your aspirations? What realistically can you do to improve the situation?
- What are the strengths and virtues of your team or organisation's culture, and what are the areas to improve?

What next?

Read *Organisational Culture and Leadership* by Edgar Schein.

42

Sandberg's *Lean In*

The power of difference

The big picture

A focus on diversity, equality and inclusion (DEI) is now an established principle of fair and effective workplaces. There is a body of research showing conclusively that engaging a range of people with a range of experiences is a positive not just for the individuals concerned, but also for organisational performance and success. The impact and benefits are clear.

With hindsight, it seems remarkable that this principle has taken so long to be recognised. And in some organisations, progress is still patchy at best. For most, DEI is still a work in progress, even where it's well established that an overreliance on people who look, think and behave the same way leaves businesses exposed to change and challenge.

One of the most significant interventions in the field of DEI came from Sheryl Sandberg, first Chief Operating Officer of Facebook (and then Meta) from 2008 to 2022 and the author of *Lean In: Women Work and the Will to Lead*. The book was an instant bestseller and has become synonymous with female empowerment, equality and the need to overcome the barriers facing women at work and beyond.

The book also led to the establishment of the Lean In Foundation, a non-profit organisation dedicated to supporting women in the pursuit of their goals and giving impetus to a much-needed conversation about gender inequality.

About the idea

In *Lean In*, Sandberg argues that gender inequality exists and that there are different types of barriers that prevent women from taking leadership roles – some subtle and cultural, some blatant and sexist, and all discriminatory and unacceptable. Sandberg also argues that there are acts of self-sabotage by women – for example, accepting discrimination, accepting gender roles and simply not speaking up – which perpetuate the problem.

A core principle of Sandberg's *Lean In* is that for change to happen, women need to break traditional societal, corporate and personal barriers by striving for leadership roles. Only by reaching and "leaning in" to leadership roles will there be more opportunities for other women, which in turn leads to greater equality and a more even gender split in organisations (and at home for family care). The benefits are huge: creating permanent systemic change leads to a fairer society, an important part of which is more successful organisations with greater market returns and better practices.

While the principle of Sandberg's *Lean In* is centred on the barriers preventing women from taking leading roles at work, the ideas also have a resonance beyond gender to other areas of bias and inequality, such as ethnicity, age, sexuality and neurodiversity.

A significant principle at the heart of *Lean In* is that if individuals break the perceived norms and raise questions, doing things differently and working together to support one another, then change will happen. More people working together, questioning norms and supporting one another will create change and drive progress. Diversity and inclusion perpetuate this progress and growth which can be personal, organisational and cultural.

Since the book's publication, the idea that it is the primary responsibility of women themselves (or any other underrepresented group) to lean in and effect change has been challenged. The notion that women can succeed through determined ambition and hard work assumed that organisations would recognise and reward them accordingly, which many have claimed has not been the case. There is a much greater acceptance that achieving equality, diversity and inclusion at work must be based on systemic and behavioural change across organisations to create the conditions in which inclusion can thrive.

However, Sandberg's work remains an influential staging post, shining a light on the crucial issue of gender inequality and offering practical support to challenge the status quo and create better, more diverse and inclusive organisations.

In practice

The essence of Sandberg's *Lean In* can be summarised in two key points.

1. The book encourages women to take an active role in their careers, assert themselves and pursue leadership positions.
2. It emphasises the importance of overcoming internal barriers, such as self-doubt, and that women should advocate for themselves to achieve professional success and gender equality in the workplace.

There are several things anyone – female or male – can do to lean in at work, and to create the climate where others can lean in too.

Build your skills and expertise. Take on new challenges and opportunities to learn and grow, developing the skills and knowledge you need to succeed in your chosen field. Identify your goals and create a plan.

Support others. While you are rising, support others and create change.

Foster diversity and inclusion. Create and nurture a culture where everyone is included and can contribute.

Seek out mentors and sponsors (and be one yourself). It can be helpful to have supportive individuals who can provide guidance, advice and advocacy on your behalf.

Network and build relationships. Relationships with others in your field can help you uncover new opportunities, as well as enabling you to gain valuable insights and advice.

Ask (and negotiate) for what you want. This could involve negotiating a pay rise, a promotion or better working conditions. It is important to be prepared and to communicate your value and impact clearly.

Substantiate change. Look around you as you progress, use your power and influence to question.

Question everything. Avoid becoming institutionalised, and look to improve the situation for yourself, your colleagues and your organisation.

Thought starters

- Does your organisation have an inclusive culture? How could it improve?
- Is there practical action that you could take in your team or organisation to help people (perhaps those lacking in confidence or feeling marginalised) to find their voice and express their ideas?
- How diverse is your thinking and your team?
- What are some of the barriers that women (or other underrepresented groups) face in your workplace, and how can they be addressed?
- Are you doing enough to support and value difference?

What next?

Read *Lean In: Women, Work, and the Will to Lead* by Sheryl Sandberg.

43

The Thomas–Kilmann conflict model

How to build influence and find agreement

The big picture

Conflict is an inevitable part of work, partly arising from the competitive, changing nature of work – what economist Joseph Schumpeter termed "gales of creative destruction" – and partly from human nature. People have always wanted agency, the ability to get their own way, or at least to influence an outcome. Historically, hierarchy, formality and power acted to dampen conflict in organisations, but the consequences of engaging more people, empowering them, more flexible working and fast-changing, uncertain times – as well as basic societal shifts – have combined to erode this hierarchy and formality. In this context the ability to influence, to provide both support and challenge, and to manage creative conflict is more important than ever.

The Thomas–Kilmann conflict model (also known as the Thomas–Kilmann conflict mode instrument, TKI) was established in 1974 by Kenneth Thomas and Ralph Kilmann, based on their research into conflict resolution and management. It is a framework that helps people understand their preferred styles of conflict resolution and offers strategies for building influence and finding agreement.

It is based on two dimensions:

1. *assertiveness:* the extent to which you try to satisfy your own concerns

2. *cooperativeness:* the extent to which you try to satisfy the concerns of others.

Based on these dimensions, the model identifies five primary styles of resolving conflict. Its aim is to help people to understand their own preferred style, and that of others, to support better conflict resolution. It also helps people to move beyond their default style, as appropriate, to listen actively, focus on interests, ensure clear communication and ultimately seek win–win solutions (see Chapter 50).

About the idea

The two key dimensions of the Thomas–Kilmann conflict model – assertiveness and cooperativeness – tend to manifest themselves in these key ways.

Assertiveness

People with a *high level of assertiveness* actively assert their preferences, desires or opinions, often seeking to achieve their objectives.

People with a *low level of assertiveness* tend to be more passive, yielding their own needs and concerns to others, and avoiding confrontation.

Cooperativeness

People with a *high level of cooperativeness* actively work towards finding solutions that meet the needs and concerns of all parties involved. They prioritise collaboration and seek win–win outcomes.

People with a *low level of cooperativeness* tend to be less concerned about the needs of others and are more focused on their own objectives.

Based on these two dimensions, the Thomas–Kilmann conflict model identifies five distinct conflict resolution styles.

1. *Competing (high assertiveness, low cooperativeness).* Competing individuals are assertive and pursue their own interests vigorously, often at the expense of others. They may use power, authority or dominance to win their position in a conflict.

2. *Collaborating (high assertiveness, high cooperativeness).* Collaborators are assertive and cooperative. They actively work with others to find solutions that meet the needs and concerns of all parties involved. Collaboration involves open communication, active listening and creative problem-solving.

3. *Compromising (moderate assertiveness, moderate cooperativeness).* Compromisers seek to find a middle ground by making concessions on both sides. They aim for an outcome that partially satisfies the needs of all parties involved.

4. *Avoiding (low assertiveness, low cooperativeness).* Avoiders try to sidestep or ignore conflicts altogether. They may withdraw from the situation or delay addressing the issue, hoping it will resolve itself over time.

5. *Accommodating (low assertiveness, high cooperativeness).* Those who accommodate will prioritise the concerns of others over their own. They are willing to yield to others' preferences to maintain harmony and preserve relationships.

Each conflict resolution style has its strengths and weaknesses, and the appropriate style to use depends on the specific situation and the individuals involved. By understanding their own and others' conflict resolution preferences, individuals can better navigate conflicts, build influence, and find agreement in various contexts, including workplaces, personal relationships and group dynamics.

Like all diagnostics that identify personal preferences, there's a danger that people feel "labelled" or stuck in one particular style. But provided that people are aware of this pitfall, the TKI can be a valuable tool for identifying default preferences, encouraging preference flexing where necessary, and promoting effective conflict management and resolution.

In practice

The Thomas–Kilmann conflict model is used to improve conflict management and resolution in various settings, such as workplaces, teams, personal relationships and organisations.

If you think the model could help you and your team, you could invest in a formal TKI assessment (you'll find a link below). You could also do some more informal reflection.

Consider your own default conflict style

Reflect on your typical responses to conflict based on the styles identified by the model. Where do you sit on the assertiveness–cooperativeness scale? Do you tend to compete or collaborate; compromise, avoid or accommodate? What are the benefits and risks associated with that style?

Develop your awareness of others

Observe the behaviour of others during conflict and try to identify their preferred conflict resolution styles. Pay attention to how they handle disagreements and interact with others.

Then, when a conflict arises, take the following steps.

Take time to analyse it

When faced with a conflict, take a moment to analyse the situation. Identify the underlying issues, interests and concerns of all parties involved. Consider the importance of the relationship and the potential impact of the conflict on it.

Choose the most appropriate conflict resolution style

If it's your job to tackle the conflict, use your analysis of the conflict and your understanding of the preferences of the involved parties to select the conflict resolution style that is most suitable for the situation. Recognise that different conflicts may require different approaches.

Even if you're just an observer, practice thinking through how you would act if you had to do so.

Communicate

When dealing with conflict, engage in open, honest and respectful communication with the other party or parties. Express your thoughts, feelings and concerns clearly while actively listening to the perspectives of others.

Be flexible

Be willing to adapt your conflict resolution style as the situation evolves. If your initial approach doesn't lead to a positive outcome, consider trying a different style to address the conflict effectively.

Aim for win–win solutions

Strive to find solutions that meet the needs and concerns of all parties involved. Collaborative and compromising styles are often effective in achieving win–win outcomes.

Manage your emotions and practice empathy and understanding

Be mindful of your emotions during conflicts and avoid reacting impulsively. Emotional regulation can lead to more rational and constructive decision making.

Put yourself in the shoes of others to understand their viewpoints and feelings better. Empathy can foster a more constructive and empathetic approach to resolving conflicts.

Use mediation if necessary

In complex or long-standing conflicts, consider involving a neutral third party to mediate the situation. A mediator can help facilitate communication, promote understanding, and guide parties toward a resolution.

Learn from each conflict

After resolving a conflict, take the opportunity to reflect on the process and outcomes. Assess what worked well and what could be improved in future conflict situations.

Thought starters

- How do you typically respond to conflict?
- Have you thought about other people's preferences when responding to conflict?
- Can you change your responses to conflict depending on the situation?
- What does win–win look like for you?
- Consider the different kinds of conflict you have to deal with and how adapting your style may lead to better outcomes.

What next?

Visit the Kilmann Diagnostics website for more information and to see the tool: www.kilmanndiagnostics.com

44

Scott's *Radical Candor*

Giving guidance that improves collaboration and results

The big picture

In her book *Radical Candor*, Kim Scott tells what she calls her "um" story.

Not long after joining Google, Scott gave a presentation to the CEO and founders of the company. Afterwards, her boss (Sheryl Sandberg, no less) offered her some feedback. Much of this was positive, but Sandberg also picked up on the fact that Scott said "um" a lot when she spoke and offered support from a speaking coach. At first Scott couldn't believe that her boss was picking up on an apparently minor thing and brushed it off. Sandberg persisted, eventually securing Scott's attention with the observation that saying "um" so much made her "sound stupid".

Scott credits the encounter with two effects. Not only did it make her want to solve her "um" problem immediately. It also made her reflect on Sandberg's style, how she combined praise and criticism to offer guidance in a way that really worked.

The encounter was just one of the many things that Scott's years of working in top tech companies in Silicon Valley contributed to her keen insight into what makes a good boss: the ability to build relationships to "guide a team to achieve results".

For Scott, bosses have three core responsibilities:

1. to create a culture of guidance that will keep people moving in the right direction
2. to understand what motivates people to keep teams cohesive

3. to drive results collaboratively. Just telling people what to do only works in certain (limited) situations.

These three factors combine to create a balance between responsibilities (the need to get things done) and relationships (doing so in a way that builds and maintains relationships). At the heart of those cultures of guidance is Scott's core idea of radical candour.

About the idea

Radical candour is the balance between two dimensions of communication.

- *Challenging directly*: being prepared to say what you need to say (and saying it clearly).
- *Caring personally*: doing so in a way that is respectful and shows that you have the other person's interests at heart.

When you *challenge directly*, you give honest feedback and hold people accountable for their actions. This can involve giving constructive criticism or recognising good performance; setting clear expectations and holding people to account if they fail to meet those expectations.

When you *care personally*, you show that you genuinely care about the person you are communicating with. This can involve expressing concern for their well-being, offering support and encouragement, and being empathetic and understanding.

By finding the right balance between these two dimensions, you are contributing to cultures of guidance that support strong, trusting relationships with colleagues.

The framework also offers a guide to what happens if this balance is off kilter.

Ruinous empathy

All care and no challenge might lead to ruinous empathy.

This can happen when you want to spare someone's short-term

Figure 8: **The balancing act behind radical candour**

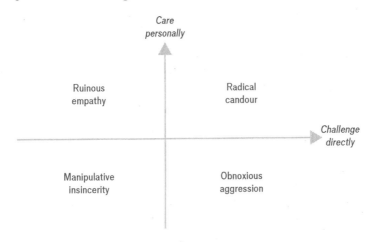

Source: From *Radical Candor: How to Get What You Want by Saying What You Mean*, first published by Macmillan in 2017, an imprint of Pan Macmillan. Reproduced by permission of Macmillan Publishers International Ltd. Text copyright © Kim Scott 2017, 2019

feelings, so you don't tell them something they need to know. It might involve praise that isn't specific enough to help the person understand what was good or less good, criticism that is sugar-coated and unclear, or even just silence. It may feel safe, but it's ultimately unhelpful and even damaging.

Obnoxious aggression

All challenge and no care move you into obnoxious aggression.

This is what happens when you challenge someone directly, but don't show you care about them personally. It's criticism and feedback that are not delivered kindly.

Manipulative insincerity

Too little of both challenge and care can come across as manipulative insincerity.

Often manifesting itself as backstabbing, politicking or

passive-aggression, this is praise that is insincere, or perhaps flattery to a person's face and harsh criticism behind their back.

Radical candour

When you balance the right amount of care with challenge, you hit the radical candour sweet spot.

Scott is clear that cultures of guidance underpinned by radical candour are not (or not only) about big set-piece *performance management* systems like formal annual appraisals. Rather, they're about regular, trust-building conversations – what Scott calls *performance development*. Cultures of guidance create working environments where feedback is a more routine part of everyday communications in the service of openness, trust-building and the kind of collaboration that drives performance.

This may sound idealistic, and Scott's thinking has certainly come in for its share of criticism. The idea has also been confused with the idea of *radical transparency,* an approach based on instant, real-time feedback where colleagues are encouraged to rate each other routinely on a range of attributes – although Scott is quite clear that this, in her terms, is obnoxious aggression writ large.

There is no doubt that striking the right balance between caring personally and challenging directly can be tricky and that getting it wrong can lead to misunderstandings and undermine, rather than create, trust. For some, the idea feels too confrontational or simply beyond the average person's self-awareness (see Chapter 2) or beyond the communication capabilities and the levels of psychological safety of the average organisation (see Chapter 5).

The need for guidance and feedback at work, however, cannot be ignored. The radical candour framework is a reminder that aspiring to better cultures of guidance is not only good for people individually, but its focus on open communication and learning also is also good for team (and ultimately organisational) performance too.

In practice

To build cultures of guidance, Scott suggests that people need to "get, give and encourage both praise and criticism". Here are some ideas to try.

Practice being open to feedback and honest about yourself

Lead by example and show you are willing to challenge yourself, hold yourself to high standards and critique your own performance.

Actively solicit feedback with open and specific "go to" questions, such as: "What more could I have done to support you on that project?" and "What's a blind spot of mine that you've noticed?" Scott acknowledges that this may feel uncomfortable, but she asks that you persist, listen and, if necessary, make changes.

Build on good performance

Remember that guidance is about building on good performance as well as course correction. Use radical candour to open up guidance conversations that go beyond a quick "well done" to reinforce and share what has worked well.

Hold colleagues accountable

Set clear expectations, let people know what being accountable means and whether there are any consequences. Then hold them accountable in a fair and transparent way.

Show that you care

Express concern and offer support and encouragement. Even when you need to have a difficult conversation, approach it with empathy and understanding. Be honest and clear, but also make sure to show that you care about the person and their well-being.

Use your own experience of feedback

Use the experience of both soliciting and receiving feedback to inform how you give feedback to others. Make it a regular part of everyday communication. Be fair, balanced, specific and forward facing. It's all about two-way conversations that help people to learn and grow.

Scott offers some top tips.

- Be humble. You may not have all the information or answers when you embark on a feedback conversation. Don't rush to judgement and explore both sides of the story.
- Be helpful. Find ways to help people to understand and meet any challenges they're facing. Be clear and specific and own what you say. Rather than saying "You're always interrupting people in meetings", try "I noticed in last week's team meeting that you interrupted Kim several times when she was trying to speak."
- Give feedback immediately. Be timely and don't let things fester.
- Where possible, give feedback in person. It's not just about what you say, but how you are heard. Giving feedback in person means you can more easily pick up on people's body language as well as what they say in response. A video call is the next best option.
- Don't personalise. When Sheryl Sandberg described Scott's "um" problem to her, she clearly said that it made her "sound stupid", not that she *was* stupid. That's an important distinction. Be as objective as possible and avoid labelling people. Say "That's wrong" rather than "You're wrong."

Thought starters

- How might you integrate some of the principles of radical candour into your own working practice? How and when might you be more radically candid?
- What are some of the potential short- and long-term problems of not addressing difficult conversations about performance or behaviour?

- What specific feedback can you give to colleagues to help them learn and improve their performance?
- How can you improve your self-awareness and understand your own communication style to help you contribute to better cultures of guidance?
- How open are you to receiving candid feedback and what are you doing to encourage it more widely?

What next?

Read *Radical Candor: How to Get What You Want by Saying What You Mean* by Kim Scott.

45

Giving great feedback

Giving fair, practical and constructive feedback

The big picture

Giving (and receiving) feedback at work can be tricky. You may know that it's important and sometimes necessary to help people to course correct or build on good performance, but it can be difficult to know where to start. It's also easy to get it wrong: to tip into confrontation, put the recipient on the defensive, fail to focus on the outcome you're trying to achieve, or duck difficult issues completely. Kim Scott's idea of radical candour can feel a bit of a stretch at times.

Having a simple framework can help. Originally developed by the Center for Creative Leadership (CCL) in the US, the situation–behaviour–impact (SBI) model is widely used to help you to craft and deliver clear, constructive and timely feedback.

SBI helps you make your feedback rigorous while also being fair and effective. It reminds you that effective feedback is a *conversation* not a monologue and must involve the other person. By focusing on behaviours rather than personalities or assumptions, it provides a clear understanding of the impact of someone's actions (or lack of action) or behaviours on others. That makes it easier for the person receiving the feedback to understand the situation and take steps to improve. It also helps the person giving the feedback to deliver it in a way that is constructive, forward facing and non-confrontational.

About the idea

The SBI model is based on the idea that feedback should be specific, objective and actionable. Therefore, it needs to be based on actual, observed behaviours rather someone's personality or assumptions about their motivations.

It involves three steps.

1. *Situation* describes the specific situation in which the behaviour occurred. This creates the context for the feedback and helps the recipient understand the specific instance being discussed. For example, start the feedback with: "During yesterday's team meeting".

2. *Behaviour* describes the specific action that took place (or did not take place). It is vital to be objective and focus on observable behaviours, rather than making assumptions or judgements about the person's intentions or character. For example, say: "I noticed that you kept interrupting others while they were speaking," or: "I'm curious as to why you didn't mention that ..."

3. *Impact* describes the impact that the behaviour had on others. Explaining the impact helps the person receiving it to understand the consequences of their behaviour and why it needs addressing. For example, say: "That behaviour made some team members feel like their opinions weren't valued, and that you had all the answers. It also disrupted the flow of the meeting and had the effect of closing down contributions."

Here is another example of using the SBI model to deliver feedback.

- *Situation:* During your presentation this morning ...
- *Behaviour:* ... I noticed that you didn't make enough eye contact with the audience, but instead read straight from your slides.
- *Impact:* I thought it made the presentation much less engaging and difficult to follow.

In these examples the feedback is specific, objective and focused on the behaviour that needs improvement. The situation sets the context for the feedback, and the impact helps the person receiving the feedback understand why their behaviour needs to change. This approach can be more effective than providing feedback that is vague or general, as it helps the person receiving the feedback understand exactly what they need to do differently in the future; it naturally opens up a conversation about what should happen next.

There are several variants to the SBI model which take a similar approach.

Situation–task–action–result (STAR) is an alternative feedback model that also focuses on a specific situation, the task/s to be carried out, describes the actions taken or not, and the results of that action, either positive or negative. An extra stage (another AR) asks the feedback giver to explore alternative actions and results that might have led to different outcomes.

Empathy-inquiry (EI) is a feedback model that emphasises the need for empathy and understanding between the two people giving and receiving feedback. It encourages the feedback giver to ask open-ended questions, and actively listen to the recipient's perspective before providing feedback. It is a useful model for building relationships and trust, and works well with deep-seated or more complicated behaviours, as well as in sensitive or fraught situations.

In practice

The SBI model offers a simple way to think about and structure a feedback conversation.

Prepare for the feedback conversation

Before giving feedback, take time to think about the specific behaviour that you observed and the impact it had. Identify a recent, significant situation where the behaviour occurred.

Think carefully about why you're giving this feedback at this time and the outcomes you want to achieve as a result of the feedback conversation.

In the conversation

Describe the situation. Start by describing the specific situation in which the behaviour occurred. This sets the context for the feedback.

Recall the behaviour. Next, describe the specific behaviour you observed. Be objective and focus on observable behaviours rather than making assumptions or judgements about the person's intentions or character.

Explain the impact. Describe the impact that the behaviour had on others, and its effects. Be specific and use concrete examples to illustrate the impact.

Work together to find a solution. The best feedback is a dialogue, not a monologue. Work with the other person to identify a solution or the next steps for them to take. Ask for their perspective and ideas on how to address any issues or to build on positives. Encourage them to take ownership of the solution and commit to making changes.

Follow up

Check in with the person regularly to see how they are doing with making changes and offer support and feedback.

Thought starters

- How could you use the SBI model to improve the feedback you give?
- How well do you understand the barriers that get in the way of effective feedback? Think about how models like SBI can help to overcome them.
- How could you use the SBI model in a coaching or mentoring context?
- How could you use the SBI model to manage change?

What next?

Read *Giving Good Feedback* by Margaret Cheng.

46

Cialdini's principles of ethical influence and persuasion

Taking the right actions for big impact

The big picture

When we talk about influence, Niccolò Machiavelli's 16th-century prince – that archetype for a scheming and cunning deployer of influence at any cost – is never far from our minds. Influencers can be seen as arch manipulators, achieving their ends by whatever means it takes, even if that means tipping over into unhealthy manipulation or abuse.

But that, according to psychologist Robert Cialdini, is to misunderstand the real power of what he calls the science of social influence. Devious or high-pressure tactics might work in the short term, but they're hardly the basis for long-term trust and cooperation.

To avoid falling into the trap of unethical influence, Cialdini suggests that we look to behavioural science. His work is based on the idea that we can persuade and influence by being mindful of "a limited set of deeply rooted human drives and needs". By understanding these, we can learn and apply some basic principles to influence effectively – and ethically.

Cialdini first shared his six principles of ethical influence and persuasion in his 1984 book *Influence: The Psychology of Persuasion*. These six (now seven) principles are a set of psychological tactics that can be used to persuade and influence others in a way that is ethical. They have been shown to be effective in a wide variety of contexts, including marketing, sales, negotiations and personal relationships.

At its simplest level, ethical influencing means explaining the benefits of a product, idea or approach and overcoming any objections. It may also mean acknowledging weaknesses or deficiencies, but pointing out that, on balance, one particular approach is preferable. It matters in many walks of life, including politics and business. And in a post-truth era of deep fakes and technology-driven influence, the work of Cialdini and others in championing ethical, fact-based approaches to decision making remains hugely significant.

About the idea

Cialdini's seven principles of ethical influence and persuasion are as follows.

1. Reciprocity: people repay in kind

People feel obliged to give back when they have received something. This principle can be used to influence others by offering them something of value first, which may then lead to a reciprocating action.

2. Consistency: people align with their commitments

If you can encourage people to commit to what you want them to do, they're much more likely to follow through. According to Cialdini, the more active, public and voluntary that commitment is, the more consistent that follow-through will be. For example, if a team member is consistently late for work, getting that person to commit (voluntarily) to a change in behaviour is likely to be more effective than pressurising them or issuing threats.

3. Social proof: people follow the lead of similar others

People are more likely to follow the actions of others in similar situations. This principle can be used to influence people by providing evidence of what others have done in similar situations. For example, businesses and consumers experience social proof through client testimonials about a product or service.

4. Authority: people defer to experts

This principle involves using the perceived authority or expertise of an individual or organisation to influence others. By establishing yourself as an expert or authority on a subject, you can use this principle to influence others.

5. Liking: people like those who like them

People are more likely to be influenced by those they like, admire or share something with. This principle can be used to influence others by building rapport and establishing common ground with them.

6. Scarcity: people want more of what they can have less of

People are more motivated to act when they believe that time or resources are limited. This principle can be used to influence others by emphasising the limited availability of a product or service, or by telling them it's a time-limited offer.

7. Unity: it's all about us

This principle involves emphasising shared identities and building a sense of community. By emphasising commonalities and creating a sense of community, individuals can use this principle to influence others. The charity sector uses this principle to build a following that shares its core belief such as wildlife conservation, disease research or inequality.

Although Cialdini's principles are based on empirical research, some critics argue that the evidence is limited, and the principles are not universal: they may not apply to all cultures and contexts. There also remains the potential for manipulation. The principles are intended to be used ethically, but some critics argue that they can be used to exploit vulnerable individuals, such as those with low self-esteem or who are susceptible to peer pressure.

Other thinking about influence includes the following.

The empathy approach to influence and persuasion involves understanding and empathising with the other person's perspective. By listening to the other person's needs and concerns, you can build trust and establish a more meaningful connection. This approach is based on the idea that people are more likely to be persuaded by those who understand and care about them.

The storytelling approach involves using stories to convey information and persuade others. By telling stories that are relevant and meaningful to the other person, you can capture their attention, imagination and engage them emotionally. This approach is based on the idea that people are more likely to be influenced by stories that resonate with them.

The social influence approach involves using social networks and communities to influence and persuade others. By leveraging social connections and networks, you can create a sense of social pressure and influence others' behaviour. This approach is based on the idea that people are more likely to conform to social norms and expectations.

The problem-solving approach involves working collaboratively with others to solve problems and find solutions. By engaging in a problem-solving process, you can build trust and establish a shared sense of purpose. This approach is based on the idea that people are more likely to be influenced by those who work with them towards a common goal.

In practice

The essence of Cialdini's principles of ethical influence and persuasion is to understand and apply psychological triggers that influence human behaviour positively, fostering relatable connections and thereby persuading others based on mutual benefit and ethical practices. The principles are typically applied when trying to influence customers, but can be equally beneficial in other contexts – for example, boosting employee engagement or change communication strategies.

Here are just some ways you might apply Cialdini's principles of ethical influence and persuasion.

Reciprocity

What can you offer that has value before asking for something in return? For example, if you want someone to review your work, offer to review theirs first.

Consistency

What active, public and voluntary commitments can you encourage people to make to show consistency that can be trusted?

Social proof

Use testimonials or endorsements from others to demonstrate the value or popularity of your product or service – or to change behaviour.

Authority

Put forward your expertise or credentials in the field to establish credibility. For example, include relevant professional qualifications on your website or social media profiles.

Liking

Build rapport and establish common ground with the other person to increase likability. For example, have informal conversations with colleagues to find that common ground, and create opportunities for cooperation and connection and to reinforce relationships.

Scarcity

Create a sense of urgency or exclusivity around your product or service to increase demand. For example, offer a limited-time discount or a limited-edition product.

Thought starters

- How can the principle of reciprocity be used to build stronger relationships with customers or clients?
- How can you use the principle of liking to improve workplace relationships and team dynamics?
- How can the principle of consistency be used to encourage individuals to make positive changes in their behaviour or habits?
- What ethical considerations should be taken into account when using Cialdini's principles of ethical influence and persuasion in marketing or advertising?
- How might the principles of ethical influence and persuasion be affected by cultural or individual differences?

What next?

Read *Influence: The Psychology of Persuasion* by Robert Cialdini.

47

Appreciative inquiry

How skilled are you at asking useful, open-ended questions?

The big picture

First developed in 1987, David Cooperrider and Suresh Srivastva's appreciative inquiry is a strengths-based approach to personal development and organisational change that builds on an individual or organisation's expertise and successes.

The premise of appreciative inquiry is that the way we frame and understand a problem or challenge significantly influences our ability to solve it or make progress. The approach uses open-ended, positive questions to explore and build upon successes and areas of expertise. It involves four key stages: discovery, dream, design and delivery.

Appreciative inquiry has been applied in a variety of settings, including businesses, non-profit organisations and community organisations. It has been used to facilitate organisational change, improve communication and collaboration, and build capacity for innovation and creativity.

About the idea

By identifying and building on strengths, appreciative inquiry invokes a collaborative process of inquiry and discovery. This helps the people involved to build on their unique strengths and capabilities. For individuals, appreciative inquiry is seen as one of the foundations of coaching. This is because of the importance of open-ended questions that are focused on developing strengths, combined with a collaborative approach which emphasises the importance of facilitating personal change and development.

Appreciative inquiry involves four key stages.

1. *Discovery*: identifying and celebrating strengths and successes. This stage is about gathering and sharing stories and examples of what is working well, and using this information to build a shared understanding of an individual's or an organisation's strengths and capabilities.
2. *Dream*: envisioning a desired future state. This is done by asking open-ended and positive questions about what could be achieved, and then using this information to create a vision of the future that is both inspiring and achievable.
3. *Design*: creating a plan to move from the current state to the desired future state. This is achieved by identifying specific actions and steps that can be taken to achieve the vision and creating a plan to implement these actions.
4. *Delivery*: focusing on implementing the plan and bringing the desired future state to fruition. This involves taking action to bring the vision to life, and continually adapting and adjusting the plan to ensure that progress is made towards the desired outcome.

These four stages are designed to be adaptable and can be customised to fit the needs and goals of an individual, organisation or community. Appreciative inquiry is often used in situations where traditional approaches to change management have not succeeded. The approach is holistic and inclusive, emphasising the importance of relationships, culture and values in achieving positive change.

Appreciative inquiry may not, of course, be the best fit for every situation. Critics argue that it is overly positive and optimistic, potentially downplaying any negative factors that should be taken into account when making decisions or effecting change. This can be problematic if there are serious issues that need to be addressed. As a result, it may not be the best approach for organisations in crisis or facing significant challenges, and it may be less effective in more hierarchical or authoritarian organisations, as it relies on participative processes that may not be feasible, or even considered desirable.

In practice

The essence of Cooperrider and Srivastva's appreciative inquiry approach is to focus on identifying and building upon strengths and positive attributes, rather than focusing solely on problems and deficits to solve problems and overcome challenges. The people involved engage in inquiry, storytelling and thinking about the future to create a desired vision and the plan to reach it.

Here's how to use appreciative inquiry in practice.

Determine the focus of the inquiry

For a company, this may be a specific business process, a particular department or a broader organisational issue. For individuals, this might be a dilemma, a decision, a relationship or a challenge.

Assemble a diverse group of stakeholders

This could include peers and other colleagues, customers, suppliers and other interested parties.

Conduct discovery interviews

These are structured conversations designed to identify and understand current strengths and successes. This is typically achieved by understanding what has worked well in the past, as well as discussing widely what is working well and ensuring success now. It helps to involve a wide and diverse range of people, and engage them with open questions that help people to reflect and describe what they feel is most valuable, and what is working well.

Analyse and synthesise the data collected

Look for patterns and themes that emerge from the discovery interviews and summarise them in a concise and meaningful way.

Develop a shared vision of the future

Based on the data collected and analysed in the previous steps, participants can envision and articulate their desired future state and what they hope to achieve through the change process.

Develop a plan

Developing a plan to move from the current state to the desired future state should be a collaborative process that involves all stakeholders and builds upon the strengths and successes identified in the discovery phase. Establish milestones and specific goals as part of the plan.

Implement the plan

Put the plan into action and work towards creating the desired future state. This may involve changes to processes, policies and structures.

Check on the progress of the change process regularly and make adjustments to the plan as needed.

Appreciative inquiry is, by design, a flexible approach that can be tailored to meet specific needs and goals. It helps to be open to new ideas and approaches, and to remain focused on the strengths and successes of the organisation throughout the process.

Thought starters

- What priority areas or issues should form the focus for appreciative inquiry?
- Where is it best to apply the principles of appreciative inquiry? Who would benefit the most?
- What relevant patterns and trends are there, and what is the most relevant, compelling vision for the future?
- Are people sufficiently open, supportive and constructive to benefit fully from this approach? Is there a risk that low morale or cynicism may undermine the process? If so, what is the solution?

- How could you use the four stages of appreciative inquiry in areas such as creative thinking or personal development planning?

What next?

Read *Appreciative Inquiry: A Positive Revolution in Change* by David Cooperrider and Diana Whitney.

48

Carnegie's *How to Win Friends and Influence People*

Mastering the art of human interaction

The big picture

Dale Carnegie's era-defining book *How to Win Friends and Influence People* was written and first published in 1936 during the Great Depression in the US – a time of economic hardship, social unrest and change.

Against this context, Carnegie's rules are a set of principles and strategies that emphasise the importance of building relationships, communication, developing interpersonal skills and finding common ground as a way of overcoming differences and achieving mutual success. The book became popular (with over 30 million copies sold worldwide) as a source of inspiration and practical advice for individuals seeking to improve their social and professional lives.

Today, Carnegie's rules remain relevant in a wide range of contexts, including business, selling, education, politics and personal relationships. The principles of effective communication, empathy and mutual respect continue to be essential skills for success in the world of work.

About the idea

Carnegie's rules for winning friends and influencing people are a set of 30 principles and strategies that include the following.

253

- Don't criticise, condemn or complain. Instead, focus on finding solutions and positive outcomes.
- Give honest and sincere appreciation. Recognise the contributions of others and show gratitude for their efforts.
- Arouse in the other person an eager want. Help others see and understand how your ideas or proposals can benefit them personally.
- Become genuinely interested in other people. Show curiosity and ask questions about others' interests, opinions and experiences.
- Smile. A smile can create a positive atmosphere and put others at ease.
- Remember that a person's name is, to that person, the sweetest and most important sound in any language. Use people's names when speaking to them to show respect and build rapport.
- Be a good listener. Encourage others to talk about themselves and their experiences and listen actively to what they have to say.
- Talk in terms of the other person's interests. Use language and examples that resonate with others' interests and experiences.
- Make the other person feel important – and do it sincerely. Recognise other people's contributions and show appreciation of their efforts.
- The only way to get the best of an argument is to avoid it. Focus on finding common ground and areas of agreement instead of arguing or criticising others.
- Show respect for the other person's opinions. Never say "You're wrong" or dismiss others' ideas outright.
- If you are wrong, admit it quickly and emphatically. Take responsibility for your mistakes and work to find solutions and make amends.

Carnegie's How to Win Friends and Influence People

- Begin in a friendly way. Create a positive and welcoming atmosphere when meeting or speaking with others.
- Get the other person to say "Yes, yes" immediately. Use questions or statements that elicit agreement and create a positive tone.
- Let the other person do a great deal of the talking. Ask open questions, seek clarification and listen actively to what they have to say.
- Let the other person feel that the idea is theirs. Encourage others to contribute their own ideas and perspectives and positively reinforce their contributions.
- Try honestly to see things from the other person's point of view. Show empathy and understanding for others' perspectives and experiences.
- Be sympathetic with the other person's ideas and desires. Recognise the motivations and interests of others, and work to find common ground and areas of agreement.
- Appeal to the nobler motives. Appeal to the other person's sense of morality and higher ideals in order to build trust and rapport.
- Dramatise your ideas. Use storytelling and vivid language to capture people's attention and create memorable messages.
- Throw down a challenge. Encourage others to take action and make positive changes and provide support and guidance to help them succeed.

For some, Carnegie's rules are firmly of their time, based on a Western, individualistic perspective that may not apply in other cultures or social contexts. Their emphasis on positivity and avoiding conflict has also been seen as unrealistic, even actively counterproductive in situations where injustice or unethical behaviour needs to be called out. Yet, somehow, over almost a century of far-reaching social, business and technological change, their simplicity and clear focus on people and relationships still manages to feel contemporary.

In practice

The essence of Carnegie's rules for winning friends and influencing people is to prioritise empathy, genuine interest and positive communication in order to build strong, long-lasting relationships, to understand other people's perspectives and achieve mutual success.

By focusing on understanding, appreciation and sincere connection, people can create a positive impact, bringing others along and inspiring innovation, collaboration and mutual success.

Carnegie's rules offer several ideas and techniques that you can use to deepen your network and build influence and connections.

Show genuine interest in the people you interact with. Ask questions, listen actively, and make an effort to understand their perspective and needs.

Be positive in your interactions. Look for opportunities to praise and appreciate others and avoid unnecessary criticism or negativity.

Find common ground – common interests or experiences that you share with others. This can help build rapport and create a sense of connection and shared experience.

Use people's names. One of the most powerful words you can use with someone is their name. Address people by their name and remember their names for future interactions. This shows that you value and respect them as individuals.

Be a good listener. Listen actively and attentively to others. This means focusing on what they are saying, asking questions, and showing that you understand and value their perspective.

Be empathetic. Try to put yourself in other people's shoes and understand their feelings and needs. Show empathy and compassion in your interactions and validate their emotions and experiences.

Communicate clearly. Be clear and concise in your communication. Avoid ambiguity or vagueness and use language that is easy to understand.

Follow up on your interactions with people, whether it is through a phone call, email, social media or in person. This shows that you value and respect their time and effort and helps to maintain the relationship over time.

Thought starters

- Think of a time when you saw or experienced someone applying one or more of Carnegie's rules. How successful was it?
- Which of Carnegie's rules might you find most helpful in your own communication and relationship-building? What is your strength? Which of Carnegie's rules could you do better – and how might you achieve this?
- How might you balance the desire to influence others with the need to remain authentic and genuine in your communications and relationships?
- How might Carnegie's rules be adapted or modified for different social and cultural contexts?
- Consider the role that empathy plays in effective communication and relationship-building. How does this relate to Carnegie's rules?

What next?

Read *How to Win Friends and Influence People* by Dale Carnegie.

49

Maister's trust equation

Building trusted relationships and partnerships

The big picture

According to author Rachel Botsman, if money is the currency of transactions, trust is the currency of interactions. If that's the case, organisations and their people clearly need both to succeed. Trust matters at work because it underpins strong, effective relationships, whether between boss and employees, between colleagues or with external stakeholders. It can also be a tricky concept to grasp. You can't simply ask people to trust you; you have to intentionally develop it with them – and it can be broken more easily than built.

The trust equation is a framework developed by business consultant and author David Maister to understand and build trust in professional relationships. The concept was first introduced in his book *The Trusted Advisor*, written with Charles Green and Robert Galford, and published in 2000.

The trust equation consists of four elements that contribute to building trust: credibility, reliability, intimacy and self-orientation. Understanding and applying the trust equation can help build trusted relationships with clients, customers and colleagues.

By demonstrating credibility, reliability and intimacy while minimising self-orientation (concern for ourselves and our own interests), people and organisations can cultivate trust, foster loyalty and create long-term, mutually beneficial partnerships. Building trust is a continuous process that requires consistent effort and genuine engagement with others.

As the world struggles with challenges including sustainability, complex supply chains and economic pressures, trust has become a key factor in transactions and relationships. It is no surprise that building trust continues to be a focus for organisations and individuals alike.

About the idea

The essence of Maister's trust equation is that trust is built on credibility, reliability and intimacy, whereas self-orientation diminishes trust. By prioritising the interest of others and demonstrating expertise, consistency and genuine care, individuals and organisations can foster strong, trusted relationships. The elements combine in the trust equation to show the level of trust that is present:

$$\text{Trust} = \frac{\text{Credibility} + \text{Reliability} + \text{Intimacy}}{\text{Self-orientation}}$$

There are four elements to "trust" in the trust equation.

1. *Credibility.* This is the perception of expertise, competence and reliability. It involves demonstrating knowledge, skills and a proven track record of delivery. Being credible means that others believe in your abilities and trust that you will fulfil your commitments effectively.

2. *Reliability.* This refers to consistency and dependability. It is about following through on promises, meeting deadlines and being accountable for your actions. When you are reliable, others can trust that you will consistently deliver what you say you will, making them feel secure and confident in the relationship.

3. *Intimacy.* In this context, intimacy does not imply a personal relationship but rather a sense of empathy, understanding and concern for others' needs and interests. Building trust involves creating a connection with others by actively listening to them, showing genuine care for people's well-being,

understanding personal and organisational challenges and being responsive to their concerns.

4. *Self-orientation.* This is the extent to which individuals and organisations focus on their own interests rather than considering the needs and concerns of others. Trust is diminished when people perceive that someone is primarily concerned about their own gains or agenda. Reducing self-orientation involves being focused on other people's needs and genuinely prioritising the other party's best interests.

Trust is built and maintained when the three elements of credibility, reliability and intimacy together outweigh self-orientation.

The trust equation has proved to be a valuable tool for people in strengthening relationships, fostering loyalty and becoming trusted advisors to their clients and colleagues.

It also reminds us that building trust is a continuing process that requires genuine engagement and a people-oriented approach to create long-lasting, mutually beneficial partnerships.

In practice

The trust equation can be used at organisational, functional and individual levels wherever there is a need to build successful, trust-based relationships – for example, with colleagues, suppliers, customers, regulators or the wider community. Here are some things to bear in mind when looking to boost your own trustworthiness.

Focus on establishing credibility

This means working on your expertise, skills and knowledge in specific areas. This can be achieved, for example, with continuing education, staying up to date with industry trends, and showcasing successful track records and case studies. Demonstrating credibility helps others believe in your abilities and builds trust in your expertise.

Be reliable and deliver on promises

To foster trust, it is essential to be consistent and dependable in fulfilling commitments. Strive to meet deadlines, deliver quality work and honour agreements. Demonstrating reliability will generate a sense of security and confidence in your ability to follow through on promises.

Demonstrate empathy and understanding

Develop a personal connection with others. Active listening and showing genuine care for the needs and concerns of others will help establish intimacy in the relationship. Be attentive to people's concerns, challenges and goals, understand their unique situations and respond with empathy.

Minimise self-orientation

Avoid focusing mainly on your own interests. Instead, prioritise the interests and goals of others. Considering others' best interests reduces self-orientation and strengthens trust.

Communicate openly and transparently

Be transparent about processes, fees and potential risks. Open communication fosters a sense of honesty and integrity, both of which are essential for building and maintaining trust.

Admit mistakes early and show accountability

Nobody is perfect and mistakes happen. When they do, it's crucial to take responsibility, apologise if necessary, and rectify the situation. Owning up to mistakes and demonstrating accountability enhances trust by showing that you value the relationship and are committed to making things right.

Be consistent

Trust is not built overnight; it requires consistent effort over time. Building and maintaining trust is a continuing process that involves nurturing relationships, delivering on promises, and consistently demonstrating reliability, credibility and intimacy. Trust is a long time in the making but can be shattered in seconds.

Reflecting on the elements of Maister's trust equation and putting them into practice can help to create lasting partnerships, and develop a reputation for integrity. Trust is the bedrock of successful relationships; actively focusing on the elements of the trust equation helps people to build better, trust-based relationships.

Thought starters

- Can you think of examples where self-orientation has undermined trust at an organisational or individual level?
- What sustained practices can you establish to ensure long-term trust?
- How do you demonstrate trust and transparency in relationships?
- How can you address situations where your self-orientation may be hindering trust-building efforts?
- What do you need to do to foster greater understanding, connection and rapport?

What next?

Read *The Trusted Advisor* by David Maister, Charles Green and Robert Galford.

50

Win–win negotiation

Radical thinking about the best way to negotiate

The big picture

Everyone needs to negotiate at work and the occasional conflict will need to be resolved in most workplaces. The idea of principled negotiation, championed by Roger Fisher and William Ury in their 1981 book *Getting to Yes*, offers a ground-breaking approach to better negotiation: a method of negotiation that looks for mutually beneficial agreement without causing conflict. This is accomplished by creating win–win outcomes for all parties. Principled negotiation is also more respectful and likely to build lasting trust. As a result, the means of negotiating are significant and beneficial, as well as the outcome.

Getting to Yes has had a significant and long-lasting impact and its principles have been adopted and adapted in negotiation training and deployment worldwide, making it a classic reference book for those seeking to improve their negotiation skills. It has influenced people in almost every work situation, smoothing the path for everything from high-end legal battles and large-scale contracts to successful pay claims or the smallest dispute about office air conditioning.

About the idea

Principled negotiation aims to resolve conflict and help people to reach agreement by focusing on mutual interest rather than adversarial positions. There are several key concepts.

Focus on interests, not positions

Instead of sticking to a specific set of demands or a fixed position, negotiators are encouraged to explore and understand the underlying interests of each party. This shift in focus helps uncover common ground, opening the way to finding creative solutions, as well as signalling that the intention is to achieve a mutually beneficial outcome that is likely to be both more valuable and durable in the longer term.

Understand best alternatives

To succeed when negotiating, it is essential to understand the best alternative to a negotiated agreement (BATNA) for all sides.

Understanding the alternatives to an agreement provides leverage, clarity and confidence during the negotiation process.

Separate people from the problem

By addressing the problem rather than making it personal, everyone can maintain a more constructive and professional discussion. That's why it is important to remove personal emotions from the negotiation.

Generate options for mutual benefit

All parties to the negotiation should brainstorm and explore as many alternatives as feasible to try to satisfy the interests of all parties. Expanding the range of possible solutions markedly increases the likelihood of generating win–win scenarios and finding an agreement that benefits everyone involved.

Create win–win solutions

These are outcomes where all parties feel they have benefited and are satisfied. This contrasts with win–lose scenarios where one party prevails at the expense of the other.

Insist on using objective criteria

Subjective opinions or arbitrary standards should be avoided. These include, for example, statements starting with "I think" (for example, "I think that won't work – my colleagues probably won't like it") or "We will" ("We will want something easier."). Instead, use objective criteria to evaluate potential solutions, as this helps to create fair and rational agreements based on widely accepted standards.

Negotiate cooperatively

Negotiation should be viewed as a joint problem-solving activity, not a zero-sum game where one party's gain is another's loss. This promotes a collaborative approach to finding a win–win solution for everyone.

In practice

The principles of principled negotiation can be applied in various practical situations to improve negotiation outcomes. Here are some examples.

Focus on interests, not positions

In your next negotiation, rather than insisting on specific terms, discuss the underlying interests. Find out why certain terms are important, and then explore creative ways to meet those interests without adhering rigidly to initial positions.

A classic example of this approach is when negotiating a price with a client. Try to find a way to meet the specific priorities of all parties. The vendor needs to make a profit and possibly establish a precedent, while the purchaser needs to achieve a solution that is affordable and may meet other needs – for example, the ability to claim to colleagues that they have secured the best available discount.

Understand best alternatives

Before a salary negotiation, assess your best alternative to a negotiated agreement – perhaps the alternative job offers or opportunities available to you or other things you might accept short of the pay rise you're looking for. This knowledge will give you confidence during negotiations, helping you make more informed decisions.

Separate people from the problem

If you're negotiating a business deal and encountering resistance, focus on the specific issues causing disagreement and at all costs avoid criticising the people involved. Discuss concerns openly, maintaining a positive and collaborative tone. This approach works well when one or more people are disagreeing about the best way forward. Stay focused on the issue, not the people.

Generate options for mutual benefit

In a team where different members have conflicting ideas, encourage brainstorming. Create a collaborative environment where team members can contribute diverse solutions, fostering creativity and finding options that can benefit everyone. Involving everyone in the process can be beneficial in itself.

Create win–win solutions

If you are working as part of a team, find solutions that benefit both the organisation and individual team members. Share tasks based on strengths and interests, fostering a positive work environment where everyone feels their contributions are valued.

Insist on using objective criteria

If you are negotiating a settlement, rely on objective standards such as legal precedents or industry benchmarks. Using firm data helps both parties see the reasoning behind proposed solutions, making agreements more grounded.

Negotiate cooperatively

Building a positive relationship contributes to successful long-term agreements. Examples include negotiating the acquisition of a business, where it is invariably best to emphasise shared interests and collaborate on solutions that address both parties' concerns.

Remember: applying the techniques of win–win negotiation means adapting these principles to the specific context of your negotiation. Flexibility, active listening and a commitment to finding common ground are key components for successful implementation. Whether at work or elsewhere, these principles provide a framework for achieving mutually beneficial outcomes.

Thought starters

- How might an awareness of principled negotiation affect and change your negotiation strategies?
- What conflict situations can you reframe as opportunities for mutual benefit? How does this change the lens of the conflict situation?
- What are the challenges to applying principled negotiation to everyday life?
- What past negotiation would have gone better if you had applied principled negotiation techniques?

What next?

Read *Getting to Yes* by Roger Fisher and William Ury.

Acknowledgements

Writing a book is never a solitary endeavour, especially with two authors. And, in this case, the book couldn't have happened without the thought leadership, innovation, thinking, collaboration and sheer brilliance of the original authors of these ideas.

To the authors, innovators, subject matter experts, professors and innovators: we thank you and extend our deepest appreciation to you all for those ground-breaking ideas which have shaped the landscape of the modern workplace. These 50 ideas are just that – the first 50 of an exceedingly long list. This book is the culmination of numerous contributions, support and inspiration from a multitude of individuals; we find ourselves overwhelmed with gratitude towards those who have made this possible and their generosity of spirit.

We are also immensely grateful to our immediate and extended families for their unwavering encouragement, patience and understanding throughout the writing process. Your love and support have meant more to us through dark days and bright than you'll ever know.

To our friends and colleagues: your insights, perspectives and feedback have enriched this book and made it stronger. Thank you.

We could not have done this without the endless encouragement, feedback, support, expertise, dedication and enthusiasm of Clare Grist Taylor at Profile Books, who should perhaps be named as the third author. Clare's professionalism and commitment to excellence has been instrumental in transforming ideas into reality.

Last but certainly not least, we extend our heartfelt appreciation to the readers of this book. This book is for you and your colleagues and your friends. Your curiosity, passion and commitment to lifelong learning are the driving force behind the continuous evolution of the world of work. It is our sincere hope that the ideas presented in this book will support, help inspire, provoke and spark meaningful insights and conversations about what you do and how you do it.

Our thanks to each and every individual who has played a part, no matter how small, in bringing *50 Ideas That Changed the World of Work* to life.

Bibliography, further reading and resources

Introduction

Frederick Winslow Taylor, *The Principles of Scientific Management* (Martino Fine Books, 2014 reprint of 2011 edition)

Ideas 1–9: The psychology of people and performance

Richard Bandler and John Grinder, *Reframing: Neuro-Linguistic Programming and the Transformation of Meaning* (Real People Press, 1983)

Patricia Bossons, Jeremy Kourdi and Denis Sartain, *Coaching Essentials: Practical, Proven Techniques for World-Class Executive Coaching* (Bloomsbury, 2012)

Isabel Briggs Myers and Peter Myers, *Gifts Differing: Understanding Personality Type* (Davies-Black, 1995)

Timothy R. Clark, *The 4 Stages of Psychological Safety: Defining the Path to Inclusion and Innovation* (Berrett-Koehler, 2020)

Mihaly Csikszentmihalyi, *Flow. The Psychology of Optimal Experience* (Harper & Row, 1990)

Mihaly Csikszentmihalyi, *Flow: The Psychology of Happiness* (Rider, 2002)

Carol Dweck, *Mindset: The New Psychology of Success* (Random House, 2006)

Carol Dweck, *Mindset: How You Can Fulfil Your Potential* (Robinson, 2012)

Carol Dweck, "Developing a growth mindset", YouTube

Amy C. Edmondson, *The Fearless Organization: Creating Psychological Safety in the Workplace for Learning, Innovation and Growth* (Wiley, 2018)

Daniel Goleman, *Emotional Intelligence: Why It Can Matter More Than IQ* (Bantam, 1995; Bloomsbury, 2020)

Daniel Goleman, *Working with Emotional Intelligence* (Bloomsbury, 1999)

Daniel Goleman, *Social Intelligence: The New Science of Human Relationships* (Arrow, 2007)

Daniel Goleman, Robert Steven Kaplan, Susan David and Tasha Eurich, *Self-Awareness*, HBR Emotional Intelligence Series (Harvard Business Review Press, 2018)

Adam Grant, *Think Again: The Power of Knowing What You Don't Know* (WH Allen, 2023)

C.G. Jung, *Psychologische Typen* (Rascher Verlag, 1921), published in English as *Psychological Types*, Volume 6 in *The Collected Works of C.G. Jung* (Routledge Classics, 2016)

William A. Kahn, "Psychological conditions of personal engagement and disengagement at work", *Academy of Management Journal*, 33(4) (1990)

Daniel Kahneman, *Thinking, Fast and Slow* (Farrar, Straus and Giroux, 2011; Penguin, 2012)

Daniel Kahneman, Olivier Sibony and Cass R, Sunstein, *Noise: A Flaw in Human Judgment* (William Collins, 2021)

Jeremy Kourdi, *Coaching Questions for Every Situation: A Leader's Guide to Asking Powerful Questions for Breakthrough Results* (Nicholas Brealey, 2021)

J. Luft and H. Ingham, "The Johari window: a graphic model of interpersonal awareness", *Proceedings of the Western Training Laboratory in Group Development*, Los Angeles, University of California (1955)

Myers Briggs Company: www.themyersbriggs.com

John Whitmore, *Coaching for Performance: The Principles and Practice of Coaching and Leadership* (Nicholas Brealey, 1992; 2024)

Ideas 10–16: Future thinking – opportunity, challenge and change

Mehrdad Baghai, Stephen Coley and David White, *The Alchemy of Growth: Practical Insights for Building the Enduring Enterprise* (Basic Books, 2000)

Warren Bennis and Burt Nanus, *Leaders: Strategies for Taking Charge* (HarperCollins, 1985)

James Clear, *Atomic Habits: An Easy & Proven Way to Build Good Habits & Break Bad Ones* (Random House Business, 2018)

Stephen R. Covey, *The 7 Habits of Highly Effective People* (Free Press, 1989; Simon & Schuster, 2020)

Stephen R. Covey, *The 8th Habit: From Effectiveness to Greatness* (Free Press, 2004)

R.B. Duncan, "The ambidextrous organization: designing dual structures for innovation", *Management of Organization*, 1 (1976)

Spencer Johnson, *Who Moved My Cheese? An Amazing Way to Deal with Change in Your Work and in Your Life* (Vermilion, 1999)

John Kotter, *Leading Change* (Harvard Business School Press, 1996; 2012)

John Kotter and Holger Rathgeber, *Our Iceberg is Melting: Changing and Succeeding Under Any Conditions* (Macmillan, 2017)

Charles A O'Reilly and Michael L Tushman, "The ambidextrous organization", *Harvard Business Review*, 82(4) (2004)

Charles A O'Reilly and Michael L Tushman, *Lead and Disrupt: How to Solve the Innovator's Dilemma* (Stanford Business Books, 2021)

Gill Ringland, *Scenario Planning: Managing for the Future* (Wiley, 2007)

Peter Schwartz, *Art of the Long View: Planning for the Future in an Uncertain World* (Wiley, 1997)

Nassim Nicholas Taleb, *The Black Swan: The Impact of the Highly Improbable* (Random House, 2007; Penguin, 2010)

Brian Tracy, *Eat That Frog! Get More of the Important Things Done Today* (Yellow Kite, 2013)

Kees van der Heijden, *Scenarios: The Art of Strategic Conversation* (Wiley, 2004)

Michele Wucker, *The Gray Rhino: How to Recognize and Act on the Obvious Dangers We Ignore* (St Martin's Press, 2016)

Ideas 17–25: The forces shaping organisations – strategy and operations

Balanced Scorecard Institute: www.balancedscorecard.org

Dan Ciampa, *Total Quality: A User's Guide for Implementation* (Addison-Wesley, 1992)

W. Edwards Deming, *The Essential Deming: Leadership Principles from the Father of Quality* (McGraw-Hill, 2013)

Robert Greene, *The 48 Laws of Power* (Profile Books, 2000)

Rita Gunther McGrath, *The End of Competitive Advantage: How to Keep Your Strategy Moving as Fast as Your Business* (Harvard Business Review Press, 2013)

Charles Handy, *The Age of Unreason: New Thinking for a New World* (Random House, 2002)

Charles Handy, *Understanding Organizations* (Penguin, 1993)

Robert S. Kaplan and David P. Norton, *The Balanced Scorecard: Measures That Drive Performance* (Harvard Business Review Press, 1996)

W. Chan Kim and Renée Mauborgne, "Blue ocean strategy", *Harvard Business Review*, 82(10) (2004)

W. Chan Kim and Renée Mauborgne, *Blue Ocean Strategy: How to Create Uncontested Market Space and Make the Competition Irrelevant* (Harvard Business Review Press, 2015)

W. Chan Kim and Renée Mauborgne, *Blue Ocean Shift: Beyond Competing: Proven Steps to Inspire Confidence and Seize New Growth* (Pan, 2022)

W. Chan Kim and Renée Mauborgne, *Beyond Disruption: Innovate and Achieve Growth without Displacing Industries, Companies, or Jobs* (Harvard Business Review Press, 2023)

A.G. Lafley and Roger L. Martin, *Playing to Win: How Strategy Really Works* (Harvard Business Review Press, 2013)

Donella H. Meadows, *Thinking in Systems* (Diana Wright, ed.) (Chelsea Green Publishing, 2017)

Alexander Osterwalder and Yves Pigneur, *Business Model Generation: A Handbook for Visionaries, Game Changers and Challengers* (Wiley, 2010)

M.E. Porter, "How competitive forces shape strategy", *Harvard Business Review*, 57(2) (1979)

Michael E. Porter, *Competitive Strategy: Techniques for Analyzing Industries and Competitors* (Free Press, 2004)

Richard Rumelt, *Good Strategy/Bad Strategy: The Difference and Why It Matters* (Profile Books, 2017)

Peter Thiel with Blake Masters, *Zero to One: Notes on Start Ups, or How to Build the Future* (Virgin Books, 2015)

Sun Tzu, *The Art of War* (Tribeca Press, 2010)

Mind Tools, "How to use SWOT analysis", video

Ideas 26–32: Going for growth – innovation, products, customers and markets

Josh Anon and Carlos González de Villaumbrosia, *The Product Book: How to Become a Great Product Manager* (Product School, 2018)

Clayton M. Christensen, *The Innovator's Dilemma: When New Technologies Cause Great Firms to Fail* (Harvard Business School Press, 1997; Harvard Business Review Press, 2024)

Clayton M. Christensen, Taddy Hall, Karen Dillon and David S. Duncan, *Competing Against Luck: The Story of Innovation and Customer Choice* (Harper Business, 2016)

Malcolm Gladwell, *The Tipping Point: How Little Things Can Make a Big Difference* (Little Brown, 2000; Abacus, 2002)

Bruce Henderson, "The product portfolio", BCG Publications, January 1st 1970, www.bcg.com

Tom Kelley, *The Art of Innovation: Lessons in Creativity from IDEO, America's Leading Design Firm* (Profile Books, 2016)

Larry Keeley, Helen Walters, Ryan Pikkel and Brian Quinn, *Ten*

Types of Innovation: The Discipline of Building Breakthroughs (Wiley, 2013)

Philip Kotler, *Marketing Management: Analysis, Planning, Implementation and Control* (Prentice-Hall, 1967)

Philip Kotler, Kevin Lane Keller, Mairead Brady, Malcolm Goodman and Torben Hansen, *Marketing Management* (Pearson, 2019)

Philip Kotler, Gary Armstrong and Sridhar Balasubramanian, *Principles of Marketing* (Pearson, 2023)

Martin Newman, *The Power of Customer Experience: How to Use Customer-centricity to Drive Sales and Profitability* (Kogan Page, 2021)

Martin Reeves, Sandy Moose and Thijs Venema, "BCG classics revisited: the growth share matrix", BCG Publications, June 14th 2014, www.bcg.com

Fred Reichheld, *The Ultimate Question: Driving Good Profits and True Growth* (Harvard Business Review Press, 2006)

Fred Reichheld, *Winning on Purpose: The Unbeatable Strategy of Loving Customers* (Harvard Business Review Press, 2021)

Ideas 33–42: Why should anyone be led by you? Leadership and teams at work

James Ashton, *The Nine Types of Leader: How the Leaders of Tomorrow Can Learn from the Leaders of Today* (Kogan Page, 2021)

Belbin resources: www.Belbin.com

R. Meredith Belbin, *Management Teams: Why They Succeed or Fail* (Routledge, 2010)

R. Meredith Belbin and Victoria Brown, *Team Roles at Work* (Routledge, 2022)

Center for Leadership Studies, situational.com

Ram Charan, Stephen Drotter and James Noel, *The Leadership Pipeline: Developing Leaders in the Digital Age* (Jossey-Bass, 2001; with Kent Jonasen, Wiley, 2024)

Caroline Criado Perez, *Invisible Women: Exposing Data Bias in a World Designed for Men* (Vintage, 2020)

J. Richard Hackman, *Leading Teams: Setting the Stage for Great Performances* (Harvard Business Review Press, 2002)

P. Hersey and K.H. Blanchard, "Life cycle theory of leadership", *Training & Development Journal*, 23(5) (1969)

Patrick M. Lencioni, *The Five Dysfunctions of a Team: A Leadership Fable* (Wiley, 2002)

Kurt Lewin, "Experiments in social space", *Harvard Educational Review*, 9 (1939)

Edwin A. Locke, "Toward a theory of task motivation and incentives", Organizational Behavior and Human Performance, 3(2) (1968)

Abraham H. Maslow, "A theory of human motivation", *Psychological Review*, 50(4) (1943)

Abraham H. Maslow, *Toward a Psychology of Being* (General Press, 2022)

Daniel H. Pink, *Drive: The Surprising Truth About What Motivates Us* (Riverhead, 2009; Canongate Books, 2011)

Sheryl Sandberg, *Lean In: Women, Work, and the Will to Lead* (WH Allen, 2015)

Edgar H. Schein, *Organisational Culture and Leadership* (Jossey-Bass, 1985; Wiley, 2016)

Simon Sinek, *Leaders Eat Last: Why Some Teams Pull Together and Others Don't* (Penguin, 2017)

Simon Sinek, *Start with Why: How Great Leaders Inspire Everyone to Take Action* (Penguin, 2011)

Brian Tracy, *Goals! How To Get Everything You Want – Faster Than You Ever Thought Possible* (Berrett-Koehler, 2010)

Bruce Tuckman, "Developmental sequence in small groups", *Psychological Bulletin*, 63(6) (1965)

Richard Whittington, Duncan Angwin, Patrick Regnér, Gerry Johnson and Kevan Scholes, *Fundamentals of Strategy* (Pearson, 2023)

Lucy Widdowson and Paul J Barbour, *Building Top-Performing Teams: A Practical Guide to Team Coaching to Improve*

Collaboration and Drive Organizational Success (Kogan Page, 2021)

Ideas 43–50: Building community and connection – relationships and influence

Rachel Botsman, *Who Can You Trust? How Technology Brought Us Together – and Why It Could Drive Us Apart* (Penguin, 2018)

Brené Brown, *Dare to Lead: Brave Work. Tough Conversations. Whole Hearts* (Vermilion, 2018)

Dale Carnegie, *How to Win Friends & Influence People* (Simon & Schuster, 1936; Westland Books, 2023)

Margaret Cheng, *Giving Good Feedback* (Profile Books, 2023)

Robert B. Cialdini, *Influence: The Psychology of Persuasion* (William Morrow, 1984; Harper Business, 2021)

Robert B. Cialdini, *Pre-Suasion: A Revolutionary Way to Influence and Persuade* (Simon & Schuster, 2016)

David L. Cooperrider and Suresh Srivastva, "Appreciative inquiry in organizational life", *Research in Organizational Change and Development* 1(1) (1987)

David L. Cooperrider and Diana Whitney, *Appreciative Inquiry: A Positive Revolution in Change* (Berrett-Koehler, 2005)

David L. Cooperrider, Diana Whitney and Jacqueline M. Stavros, *Appreciative Inquiry Handbook: For Leaders of Change* (Berrett-Koehler, 2008)

Stephen M.R. Covey and Rebecca R. Merrill, *The Speed of Trust: The One Thing That Changes Everything* (Free Press, 2008)

Roger Fisher and William Ury, *Getting to Yes: Negotiating Agreement Without Giving In* (Houghton Mifflin, 1981; Penguin, 2011)

Therese Huston, *Let's Talk: Make Effective Feedback Your Superpower* (Penguin, 2022)

Kilmann Diagnostics: kilmanndiagnostics.com

Ralph H. Kilmann, *Mastering the Thomas–Kilmann Conflict Mode Instrument* (Kilmann Diagnostics, 2023)

Paul McGee, *How to Speak So People Really Listen: The*

Bibliography, further reading and resources

Straight-Talking Guide to Communicating with Influence and Impact (Capstone, 2016)

David H. Maister, Charles H. Green and Robert M. Galford, *The Trusted Advisor* (Free Press, 2000; 2021)

Steve Martin, *Influence at Work* (Profile Books, 2024)

Kim Scott, *Radical Candor: How to Get What You Want by Saying What You Mean* (Pan, 2019)

Douglas Stone and Sheila Heen, *Thanks for the Feedback: The Science and Art of Receiving Feedback Well* (Penguin, 2015)

William Ury, *Getting Past No: Negotiating in Difficult Situations* (Bantam, 1993)

We'd love to hear from you

We are keen to hear your feedback, as well as your own suggestions for ideas that are changing the world of work. Please join our LinkedIn community where we'll discuss how work is changing, progressing and improving.

Please visit //50ideas.world

Please visit:
www.linkedin.com/company/50-ideas/

Index

7 Habits of Highly Effective People: Powerful Lessons in Personal Change (Stephen R. Covey) 81–4
8th Habit, The: From Effectiveness to Greatness (Stephen R. Covey) 83, 84
9/11 56
2008 financial crisis 56

A
accommodation 227
accountability 235, 261
achievement 208
acronyms, miscellaneous 206
action 48, 191
active listening 25
adaptability 53, 105
Age of Unreason, The: New Thinking for a New World (Charles Handy) 113, 117
agency 49, 225
aggression 233, 234
agile 137–8
Aguilar, Francis 107
air fryers 96–7
Airbnb 90, 141
airlines 88, 91, 142–3, 146
Alchemy of Growth, The (Baghai, Coley and White) 63
alignment 78, 207

"allowable weaknesses" 190
see also weaknesses
alternative products 96–7
Amazon 66, 90
ambidexterity 63–8
nature of 63
"ambidextrous organization, The" (Charles O'Reilly and Michael Tushman) 68
ambiguity 52, 54, 205
anchoring 14, 15
anger 7, 8
Ansoff matrix 147
anxiety 8
Apple
ambidexterity 67
disruptive businesses 90
iPod 143
smartphones 153
VUCA 54
appreciative inquiry 248–52
Appreciative Inquiry: A Positive Revolution in Change (David Cooperrider and Diana Whitney) 252
approval, seeking that of others 20
archaic innovation 144
architects 19
Art of War, The (Sun Tzu) 85–9

artifacts 216
Ashton, James 177
assertiveness 29, 225, 226–7
assumptions 216
Australia 56
authenticity, personal 41
autonomy 212
autotelic experiences 46, 48
avoiders 227
awareness 48, 228
 see also self-awareness

B
Baghai, Mehrdad 63
Bain & Company 158
balanced scorecards (BSC)
 128–34
 Institute website 134
 perspectives of 129
Bandler, Richard 13, 16
basic underlying assumptions
 216
BATNA (best alternative to a
 negotiated agreement) 264
"BCG classics revisited: the
 growth share matrix" (Martin
 Reeves, Sandy Moose and
 Thijs Venema)
BCG matrix *see* growth share
 matrix
behaviour
 anchoring 14
 anti-social 170
 blind spots 42
 challenges and 15
 customer behaviour 160
 emotional resilience and 8

language, thought and 13
leadership and 173, 175, 178,
 180, 184
MBTI and 36
of others 228
others affected by 10
patterns of 175
rather than the person 238–9
situation-behaviour-impact
 model (SBI) 238–41
systems thinking 124
in teams 189–93, 196, 202
behavioural psychology 3, 178
behavioural science 242
Belbin, Meredith 189
Belbin team roles 189–93
 nine roles 191
belonging 24
Benepe, Otis 107
Bennis, Warren 51, 54
Bezos, Jeff 66, 73
bias 4–8, 55
*Black Swan, The: The Theory of
 the Highly Improbable* (Nassim
 Nicholas Taleb) 55, 58
black swans 55–8, 60
Blanchard, Ken 178–9
blind spots 40–42, 55
blue ocean strategy 90–94
*Blue Ocean Strategy: How
 to Create Uncontested
 Market Space and Make the
 Competition Irrelevant* (Chan
 Kim and Renée Mauborgne)
 90, 94
blue oceans 90–94
boards of directors 72

Index

body language 15, 236
see also language
Boston Consulting Group
(BCG) 147, 149
Botsman, Rachel 258
brainstorming 266
brand loyalty 156, 158
Bratton, William 171
break taking 6
breakfast cereals 154
Briggs, Katharine 33
Briggs Myers, Isabel 33
building relationships
improving them 16
"secret economy" of 9
strong ones with rapport 11, 12
usefulness of 223
VUCA and 53
Building Top-Performing Teams
(Lucy Widdowson and Paul J.
Barbour) 198
bureaucracies 113, 115
business environment 52
business model canvas 101–6
Business Model Generation
(Alexander Osterwalder and
Yves Pigneur) 101, 106
business plans 102
business process re-engineering
(BPR) 118–22
definition 119
business rivals 97
business structures,
miscellaneous 115
buyers 96

C

Canon 98
carbon reduction 111
Carnegie, Dale 253–7
Carnegie's *How to Win Friends
and Influence People* 253–7
30 principles 253–5
Casella Wines 93
cash cows 148, 151
Center for Creative Leadership
(CCL) 238
Center for Leadership Studies
182
see also leadership
challenges
coaching and 27–8
different mindsets and 18
facing 19
flow and 47
identifying 138–9
overcoming 15
Champy, James 119
Chan Kim 90, 91, 141
change 17, 69–74, 87, 224
CHAOS 52
see also VUCA
Charan, Ram 183
Charan's leadership pipeline
183–8
see also leadership
charity sector 244
Cheng, Margaret 241
Christensen, Clayton 141, 142,
144, 146
Church of Jesus Christ of Latter-
Day Saints (Mormons) 81
Churchill, Winston 19

Cialdini, Robert 242
Cialdini's principles of ethical influence and persuasion 242–7
Ciampa, Dan 118
Cirque du Soleil 91
clarity 176, 200
Clinton, Bill 170
coaching 27–32, 179, 248
  coach as sounding board 31
Coaching for Performance: The Principles and Practice of Coaching and Leadership (Sir John Whitmore) 32
coffee shops 167–8
Cold War 51, 69
Coley, Stephen 63
collaboration 227
  see also teamworking
comfort zones, stepping outside 19, 21, 45
commitment 179–80, 243, 261
common ground 256, 264
communication
  between colleagues 23, 65, 92
  conflict and 229
  follow ups 256–7
  goals and 207
  internal and external 105
  situational leadership 182
  teams 202
  transparency 261
  Zoom 116
community, sense of 244
competence 179–80
competitive advantage 95–100

Competitive Strategy: Techniques for Analysing Industries and Competitors (Michael Porter) 100
complexity 52, 54
compromise 227
confidence 47, 49
conflict 225–30
connectors 170, 171
consistency 243, 246, 259, 261–2
context 170–71
continuous improvement 118, 119, 120, 145
continuous learning 25
contract workers 114, 117
control 8, 30, 47
cooperativeness 226–7
Cooperrider, David 248, 250
core functions 114, 116
cost structure 103
  fixed costs 113
Covey's seven habits of highly effective people 81–4
covid-19 56–7, 120
creative cooperation 82
"creative destruction" (Joseph Schumpeter) 136
credibility 259, 260
criminality 171
critical paths 123–7, 183–4
criticism 18
Csikszentmihalyi's flow 46–50
culture 217
  guidance from 234–5
  see also organisational culture
culture web 217–18

customers
  customer experience 136
  customer satisfaction 158–62
  giving increasing value to 100
  perspectives on 131
  segments, and relationships
    with 102
  switching products 96

D
dangerous silences 24
data 120, 139, 150, 219
decision making 3–6
  goals and 207
  improving 77
  short- and long-term 65,
    67
  uncertainty and 54
delegation 180
Deloitte's Innovation Practice
  135
Deming, Edwards 122
denial 42
dependability 259
design thinking 137
"Developing a Growth Mindset"
  (Carol Dweck) 21
development
  of focus 49
  Johari windows 41, 44
  MBTI and 33
  plans 206
  of self-awareness 9–10
  situational leadership and 181
  of skills 49, 185
  SWOT assessments 112
different points of view 5

directors 184, 186–7
disruptive innovation 141–6
  low-end disruptive innovation
    142–3
  new-market disruptive
    innovation 143–4
  see also innovation
distributed leadership
  see also leadership
distribution 164, 166
diversity 24, 25
  diversity, equality and
    inclusion (DEI) 221, 222–3
Doblin's *Ten Types of Innovation*
  135–40
dress codes 216
Drive: The Surprising Truth
  About What Motivates Us
  (Daniel Pink) 212, 214
Drotter, Stephen 183
Drucker, Peter 81, 147, 204
Duncan, Robert 63
DVDs 152, 154
Dweck, Carol 17, 19

E
easyJet 143
Eat That Frog! Get More of the
  Important Things Done Today
  (Brian Tracy) 80
Edmondson, Professor Amy
  22–5
effectiveness 81–4, 177
efficiency 120
effort 18
effortlessness 48
ego 47

eight steps for leading change
70–74
Eisenhower, Dwight D. 75
Eisenhower Matrix, The 75–80
electric vehicles (EVs) 153
emergence 124
emotional intelligence 7–12
Emotional Intelligence: Why It Can Matter More Than IQ (Daniel Goleman) 7, 12
emotional resilience 8, 10
emotions 7
  contagiousness of 9
  control of 8, 229
  dominant emotions 10, 11
  naming of 10
  remove from negotiations 264
  understanding of 9, 15
empathy
  benefits of 9
  caring personally 232
  Dale Carnegie 255–6, 257
  development of 11, 16
  empathy-inquiry (EI) feedback model 240
  establishing trust 259, 261
  in conflicts 229
  in influence 245
  nature of 92
  ruinous empathy 232–3
employees 2, 132, 160, 189
End of Competitive Advantage, The (Rita Gunther McGrath) 99
end results 20
enterprise managers 187
  see also managers

espoused values 216
Essential Deming, The: Leadership Principles from the Father of Quality (Edwards Deming) 122
ethical influence 242–7
  seven principles of 243–4
experts 121, 244
exploitation (in ambidexterity) 64, 65, 67
exploration (in ambidexterity) 64, 65, 67
extraverts 34

F
Facebook 145, 221
farming 62
fast and slow thinking 3–6
Fearless Organisation, The (Amy Edmondson) 22, 26
feedback 238–41
  active seeking of 235
  as a regular feature 235–6
  behaviour and situation relevant 239, 240
  the behaviour rather than the person 238–9, 240
  challenging directly 232
  checking progress 207
  coaching and 31
  effectiveness of 21
  empathy-inquiry (EI) 240
  Giving Good Feedback (Margaret Cheng) 241
  GROW method 29
  Johari window and 41, 43–4
  kaizen groups 120

on leadership 176
loops 105, 124, 126
monitoring continuous
  improvement 219
motivation from 204
Sandberg to Scott 231, 236
situation-behaviour-impact
  (SBI) model 238–40
situation-task-action-result
  (STAR) 240
Stanford method 20
states of flow and 47, 49, 50
feeling and thinking 35
financial markets 124
fixed costs 113
fixed mindsets 17, 18
flexibility 53, 177, 229, 267
flow 46–50
*Flow: The Psychology
  of Happiness* (Mihaly
  Csikszentmihalyi) 50
focus 49
FOCUS 52
  see also VUCA
Ford 141
future and the present, the 63,
  64

G
Gardner, Howard 7
gender 221–4
General Electric 183
Getting to Yes (Roger Fisher and
  William Ury) 263, 267
gig economy 115
Gladwell's tipping point
  169–72

goals 204–8
  achieving 208
  alignment of 78
  balanced scorecards and
    130–31
  clarity and realism in 85–6,
    200
  commitment 29
  communication 207
  decision making and 5, 207
  end and performance goals 28
  factors preventing
    achievement 16
  GROW model and 27–8
  identifying 14
  key metrics and measures 130
  motivation and 10, 207
  options 28, 31
  questions to ask 30
  reality in 28, 30
  setting 14, 15, 49
  systems thinking and 127
  two main types 206
  use of SWOT technique 108
*Goals! How To Get Everything
  You Want – Faster Than You
  Ever Thought Possible* (Brian
  Tracy) 208
Goleman, Daniel 7–9, 11–12, 45
Google 22, 231
Great Depression 253
*Grey Rhino, The: How to
  Recognise and Act on the
  Obvious Dangers We Ignore*
  (Michele Wucker) 56
grey rhinos 56–8
Grinder, John 13, 16

group dynamics 194, 195, 217
GROW model (coaching) 27–32
growth mindsets 17–21
growth share matrix 147–51
guidance 234–5
gut reaction 6

H
Hackman, Richard 199, 201
Hackman's enabling conditions
   for teams 199–205
   see also team working
Hammer, Michael 119
Handy, Charles 113
Harvard Business Review 90, 95
Henderson, Bruce 147
Hersey, Paul 178–9
Herzberg, Frederick 211–12
hierarchical structures
   kaizen 119
   leadership pipeline model 185
   psychological safety and 23
   shamrock organisations 113,
      115
hierarchies of needs 209–10
hindsight 3, 55
historical data 57
"histories of the future" 61
holistic approaches 124, 130
home delivery services 115
"How to use SWOT analysis"
   (Mind Tools) 112
   see also SWOT analysis
*How to Win Friends and
   Influence People* (Dale
   Carnegie) 253–7
   30 principles 253–5

hygiene 211–12

I
IBM 141
identity 64, 67
Imai, Masaaki 119
impact (of behaviour) 239
imperfections, acknowledging 19
implementation 139, 219
importance/urgency 75–7
in the moment 4
inclusion 24
incremental innovation 144
*Influence: The Psychology of
   Persuasion* (Robert Cialdini)
   242, 247
influencers 170, 171, 242
information 86
Ingham, Harrington 40
innovation 135–46
   Alchemy of Growth and 63–4
   archaic innovation 144
   disruptive innovation 138,
      141–6
   incremental innovation 144
   innovation ambition 137
   Innovation Practice
      (Deloitte's) 135
   O'Reilly and Tushman 66–7
   re-engineering processes 121
   sustaining innovation 142
   technological 92
   VUCA 2:0 52
*Innovator's Dilemma, The:
   When New Technologies Cause
   Great Firms to Fail* (Clayton
   Christensen) 146

Index

INSEAD 90
insincerity 233–4
integrity 261, 262
interdependence 124, 200, 201–2
introverts 34
intuition 3, 4, 34
iPod 143
Israeli-Arab War, 1973 59
iTunes 143

J
Japan 118
jargon 14
Jensen, Mary Ann 195
Jobs, Steve 54
Johari windows 40–45
  appropriate adjectives 43–4
  four quadrants of 41–4
Johnson, Gerry 217
judging 35
Jung, Carl 33

K
Kahn, William 22
Kahneman, Daniel 3–6
kaizen 118–22
Kaplan, Robert 128
Keeley, Larry 135, 137
key items 97, 103
key performance indicators (KPIs) 105, 159, 165, 206
Kilmann, Ralph 225
Kilmann Diagnostics website 230
Kodak 141, 152
Kongö Gumi 1

Kotler's four Ps of marketing 163–8
Kotter, John 69–74
Kotter's eight steps for leading change 69–74

L
language patterns 13–16
  behaviour, thought and 13, 16
  body language 15
  patterns 13–14, 15
leaders 23, 231–2
Leaders: Strategies for Taking Charge (Warren Bennis and Burt Nanus) 54
leadership
  Center for Creative Leadership 238
  Center for Leadership Studies 182
  for change 69–74
  Charan's leadership pipeline 183–8
  distributed leadership 185
  Kurt Lewin on 173–7
  Nine Types of Leader (James Ashton) 177
  situational leadership 178–82
  behaviourism 178
  Steve Jobs 54
  team leaders 199–200, 201
  types of 174–5
  women and 222–3
Leadership Pipeline, The: How to Build the Leadership Powered Company (Charan, Drotter and Noel) 183, 188

Leading Change (John Kotter) 69–74

Leading Teams: Setting the Stage for Great Performances (Richard Hackman) 199

lean approaches 137

Lean In: Women Work and the Will to Lead (Sheryl Sandberg) 221–4

Lean In Foundation 221

learning 92

Lewin's leadership styles 173–7

see also leadership

limited availability 244, 246

LinkedIn 88

listening 254

Locke, Edwin 204

Long Range Planning Service (Stanford Research Institute) 107

low-cost airlines *see* airlines

low-end market footholds 141, 145

see also disruptive innovation

Luft, Joseph 40

M

Machiavelli, Niccolò 242

Mahler, Walter 183

Maister, David 258

Maister's trust equation 258–62

managers 184, 185–6

enterprise managers 187

manipulation 244–5

manipulative insincerity 233–4

maps 126

market growth 147–51

market research 155

market share 147–51, 156

marketing 104, 163–8

Gladwell's tipping point 169

Marketing Management: Analysis, Planning, Implementation and Control (Philip Kotler) 163, 168

Maslow, Abraham 209

Maslow's hierarchy of needs 209–11

mastery 212

Mauborgne, Renée 90, 91, 141

mavens 170, 171

Mayer, John 7

McGrath, Rita Gunther 99

McKinsey three horizons model 63–4, 66

Meadows, Donella 127

measurement 128, 130–31, 204–5, 207

mediation 229

medical procedures 24

mentors 223

Meta 145, 221

metrics 128, 130, 165

Mind Tools 112

mindfulness 5

Mindset: The New Psychology of Success (Carol Dweck) 17

mindsets, shaping of by others 19, 29

see also fixed mindsets; growth mindsets

mistakes 120, 261

Mitchell, Arnold 107

modelling 14

momentum 71, 73

Index

mood 8
Mormons 81
motivation 209–14
    Abraham Maslow 209–10
    extrinsic and intrinsic 212
    factors in 204
    flow and 48, 49
    goals and 207
    Herzberg 211–12
    motivating others 10
    remuneration's limits 213
    self-motivation 8, 12
movers 170
music 143, 144
MVPs (minimum viable
    products) 104
Myers, Isabel Briggs 33
Myers-Briggs Type Indicators
    (MBTI) 33–9
    criticisms of 36
    Johari's window and 40
    personality types 37–8

N

Nanus, Burt 51, 54
needs 209–11
negotiation 263–7
    interests of parties not
        positions 264, 265
Net Promoter Scores (NPTs)
    158–62
Netflix 154
networking 223
neuro-linguistic programming
    (NLP) 13–16
neuroscience 3
new entrants (to a market) 95–6

new jobs 87
new-market footholds 141, 145
    see also disruptive innovation
New York 171
Nine Types of Leader, The: How
    the Leaders of Tomorrow Can
    Learn from the Leaders of
    Today (James Ashton) 177
Noel, James 183
Norton, David 128
"not yet" situations 21

O

obnoxious aggression 233, 234
obstacles 18, 28
OPEC (Organisation of
    the Petroleum Exporting
    Countries) 59
open-ended questions 248, 255
openness 41–2, 45
opinion voicing, opportunity
    for 23
opportunities 138–9
    see also SWOT analysis
optimal experience 46–7
O'Reilly, Charles 63, 66
Organisational Culture and
    Leadership (Edgar Schein)
    215–20
Osterwalder, Alexander 101, 102
overthinking 5

P

packaging 165
paralysis by analysis 5
participation 25
partnerships 165

people as social animals 7
perceiving 35
performance
  balanced scorecards 129, 132, 134
  Doblin's ten types of innovation 136
  goals 206
  managers and 186
  marketing and 165
  performance development 234
personality assessment 33
personality types 34–9
perspectives 125, 130–32
PEST analysis (political, economic, sociocultural, technological) 107–8, 111–12, 149
  PESTLE 112
Pigneur, Yves 101
Pink, Daniel 212, 214
Porter, Michael 95
Porter's five forces: competitive strategy 95–100, 147, 149
possibility 52
present and the future, the 63, 64
pricing
  competition 156
  example 167
  factors 164, 166
  negotiating 265
  sensitivity 100
Principles of Scientific Management, The (Frederick Winslow Taylor) 1–2

priorities 14, 75–80, 207
probability 58
problem-solving 6, 245, 265
processes 20, 119–20, 136, 165
product 163–4, 166, 167
Product Book, The: How to Become a Great Product Manager (Josh Anon and Carlos González de Villaumbrosia 157
product life cycle (PLC) models 152–7
"product portfolio, The" (Bruce Henderson) 147
productivity 186
profitability 100
progress 10, 207
Project Aristotle (Google) 22
promotion 164, 166–7, 168
  see also marketing
psychological danger 24
psychological safety 22–6, 66
Psychological Types (Carl Jung) 33
psychology 7, 41
pulse surveys 158
purpose 212, 218–19

R

Radical Candor: How to Get What You Want by Saying What You Mean (Kim Scott) 231, 237
radical candour 231–7, 238
  the balancing act 232–3, 234
radical transparency 234
randomness 57

Index

rapport
  building relationships 11, 12,
    16, 244
  GROW coaching and 29
  neuro-linguistic programming
    and 14
  reciprocity 243, 246
red oceans 90, 91
re-engineering 118–22
reframing 13–16, 20
*Reframing: Neuro-Linguistic
  Programming and the
  Transformation of Meaning*
  (Richard Bander and John
  Grinder) 16
Reichheld, Fred 158, 162
reliability, 259, 261
relationship building *see*
  building relationships
resilience 52, 54, 60
resource allocation 104
respect 24
rest 6
revenue streams 103, 104
risk management 57–8, 93
risk-taking 23–6, 63–6, 72–3, 175
Rogers, Carl 81
Royal Dutch Shell 59
ruinous empathy 232–3
  see also empathy

S

sadness 8
safe spaces 24
safe workplaces 25
salary negotiations 266
  see also negotiations

salespeople 170
Salovey, Peter 7
Samsung 153
Sandberg, Sheryl 221, 231, 236
Sandberg's Lean In 221–4
satisfaction 47, 212
Satmatrix 158
scale 105
scenario planning 57, 59–62
*Scenarios: The Art of Strategic
  Conversation* (Kees van der
  Heijden) 62
Schein, Edgar 215, 220
Schein's three levels of
  organisational culture 215–20
Scholes, Kevin 217
Schumpeter, Joseph 135–6, 225
Scott, Kim 231, 234, 237, 238
self 47
self-actualisation 209–10,
  211–12
self-awareness
  blind spots and 40
  cultures of guidance and 237
  development of 9–10
  emotional intelligence and 8
  fast and slow thinking 4
  helping others develop 45
  Johari windows 42
  neuro-linguistic programming
    15
  personality types and 39
  psychological techniques 41
  Self-Awareness (Daniel Goleman
    et al) 45
  self-confidence 47, 49
  self-control 8

293

self-development *see* development

self-disclosure 43–4

self-doubt 223

self-orientation 260, 261

self-regulation 8

self-worth 211

sensing 34

sensitivity 12

sequencing 125

shamrock organisations 113–17

situation-behaviour-impact (SBI) model 238–41

situation-task-action-result (STAR) 240

situational leadership 178–82
see also leadership

skills
building 223
Charan's leadership pipeline 183–4
development of 49, 185
exploration and exploitation 65
Flow and 47
teams 200

slow and fast thinking 3–6

SMART (specific, measurable, achievable, relevant, time-bound) objectives 201, 204–8

smartphones 153

social media 245

Southwest Airlines 143

sponsors 223

sport 19

Srivastva, Suresh 248, 250

stakeholders 99, 187

Stanford method (feedback) 20

Stanford Research Institute 107

stereotyping 5

Stewart, Robert 107

stickiness factor 170, 171

storytelling 16, 245

strategic management 147

strategic planning 101–6, 107

strategy 52, 85, 130

streaming 91

strengths 148, 191
see also SWOT analysis

success of others, responding to 18

Sun Tzu 85–9

sunk-cost traps 88

suppliers 96

supply chains 120, 124, 137

support 27, 41, 200, 223

surgeons 180

surveys 161

sustaining innovation 142

swans 55–6
see also black swans

SWOT analysis (Strengths, Weaknesses, Opportunities, Threats) 107–12, 149
development of 108–11

systems thinking 123–7

T

taking breaks 6

Taleb, Nassim Nicholas 55–6

Taylor, Frederick Winslow 1–2

teamworking 189–203
Belbin team roles 189–93
Building Top-Performing Teams (Lucy Widdowson and Paul J. Barbour) 198
Hackman's enabling conditions for teams 199–203
Leading Teams (Richard Hackman) 199
lone geniuses and 135
project teams 87
structure 200
team building 197, 198
team leaders 199–200
Tuckman's stages of team development 194–8
technology
Bezos at Amazon 66
blue ocean companies 92
new-market disruptive innovation 143
opportunities and threats of 109, 112
Ten Types of Innovation: The Discipline of Building Breakthroughs (Larry Keelcy) 135–40
Tesla 153
thinking and feeling 35
Thinking, Fast and Slow (Daniel Kahneman) 3, 6
Thinking in Systems (Donella Meadows) 127
Thomas, Kenneth 225
Thomas–Kilmann conflict model, the 225–30
thought 13, 16, 191, 192–3

threats *see* SWOT analysis
three horizons model (McKinsey) 63–4, 66
time 48, 205
time management 14, 75–80
Tipping Point, The: How Little Things Can Make a Big Difference (Malcolm Gladwell) 169, 170, 172
total quality management (TQM) 118, 120
"Toward a theory of task motivation and incentives" (Edwin Locke) 204
training programmes 4, 197, 198
transient competitive advantage *see* competitive advantage
trust 258–62
equation 259
Johari windows 41, 42
neuro-linguistic programming 14, 16
teams 24
Trusted Advisor, The (David Maister, Charles Green and Robert Galford) 258, 262
Tuckman, Bruce 194, 195
Tuckman's stages of team development 194–8, 199
four stages 195, 196
Tushman, Michael 63, 66

U

Uber 141, 145
Ultimate Question, The: Driving Good Profits and True Growth (Fred Reichheld) 162

uncertainty
  boosting resilience 54, 60
  covid-19 and other pandemics 57
  fear of 62
  nature of 52
underlying assumptions 216
United Nations 19
unpredictable situations 51
urgency/importance 75–7
Ury, William 263
US Army War College 51, 52

V
value 103, 216
video cassettes 152
vinyl records 144
vision 70, 72–3, 196
visualisation 14, 15, 16, 104
Vlamingh, Willem de 56
voicing opinions, opportunities for 23
volatility 52, 54
VUCA (volatility, uncertainty, complexity, ambiguity) 51–4
VUCA 2:0 52–3
VUCA Prime 52

W
Wack, Pierre 59

weaknesses 148
  see also SWOT analysis
White, David 63
Whitmore, Sir John 27–8
win-win situations 229
  negotiations 263–7
women 221–4
  leadership by 222–3
  overcoming self-doubt 223
workplaces 175, 209–10
works in progress, people as 19
Wucker, Michele 56
www.balancedscorecard.org 134
www.Belbin.com 193
www.themyersbriggs.com 39

X
Xerox 98

Y
Yellow Tail 93

Z
Zakon, Alan 147
zero tolerance 171
Zoom 116
Zuckerberg, Mark 145